A TIME FOR CHRISTIAN CANDOR

A TIME FOR

JAMES A. PIKE

CHRISTIAN CANDOR

But we have this treasure in earthen vessels,
that the excellency of the power may be of
God, and not of us.—II CORINTHIANS 4:7

HARPER & ROW, PUBLISHERS
NEW YORK, EVANSTON,
AND LONDON

TO MY SON JIM

CONTENTS

Preface and a Note on Method 7

I   WHY BELIEVE? 13

II   CREED 25

III   CODE 37

IV   CULT 51

V   WHAT CHRISTIANITY IS 58

VI   GOOD OUT OF EVIL 78

VII   GOD AND THE PARTICULAR 99

VIII   WHAT THINK YE OF CHRIST? 108

IX   HIS DEATH AND RESURRECTION 116

X   THE TRINITY 120

XI   AN APOLOGIA FOR EARTHEN VESSELS 131

6 / CONTENTS

Appendix A "TRINITY IN UNITY": REMARRIAGE IN THE EPISCOPAL CHURCH 143

Appendix B ON CERTAIN RELATIVITIES IN CULT AND POLITY 145

Appendix C ON CHRISTOLOGICAL HERESIES 151

Appendix D LITURGICAL REFORM TOWARD RELEVANT CONTINUITY 153

Index of Names and Subjects 155

Index of Scripture Quotations 160

Preface and a Note on Method

We are in the midst of a theological revolution. It is not that the present well-known attempts to rethink and restate the Christian faith are entirely original, either in approach or in content; a good deal of all this has long been in learned books and in seminary lectures. But now more than ever, the process is going on *in public*. A definitive point—both revealing as to the long course of private dialogue in this regard and causing more public expression—was the recent publication of *Honest to God* by John A. T. Robinson, Bishop of Woolwich.[1] Since its appearance, and innumerable responses in books, reviews, articles, and sermons (affirmative, negative or qualified),[2] hundreds of thousands of people, inside and outside the Church, have been affected by learning about this long and grueling revolution in Christian thinking and by reading various attempts to check or suppress it.

Quite innocently three years ago I had stirred up a more modest controversy, but one of the same genre, with an article in the *Christian Century* series, "How My Mind Has Changed."[3] Though the clergy of the Episcopal Church in South Georgia who charged me with heresy were rather few in number, a considerable public

[1] S.C.M. (U.K.), Westminster (U.S.), 1963.
[2] Reactions to the book have been collected in *The Honest to God Debate*, ed. by David Edwards and John A. T. Robinson, S.C.M. (U.K.), Westminster (U.S.), 1964.
[3] Published under the same title by World Pub. Co., 1961.

7

fanfare ensued. In the midst of this, an old friend, Eugene Exman, religious books editor of Harper & Row, and his colleague, Melvin Arnold, urged me to write a book on what I *do* believe. This I agreed to do under the title "I Believe." But the burdens of office prevented me from getting further than drafting about half the chapters. Then came a turning point: the Bishop of Woolwich was kind enough to send me an advance copy of the English edition of his *Honest to God.* His insights, his courage, and his capacity to make plain a point of view hitherto only understood by the professionals and by that particular group of laity whom we can call theological amateurs (in the best sense of the word), inspired me to think through the full implications of the positions I had heretofore taken—not only in the *Christian Century* article, but in certain portions of previous writings and with increasing explicitness in sermons and addresses, and to essay a contribution to the present work of theological reconstruction, both for professionals and for laymen who will read as they run.

Reconstruction involves some destruction as well as some construction; consequently the destruction began with the scrapping of all but one chapter of my original draft. As in the case of Dr. Robinson's book, both the negative and positive parts of the task have genuine positive purposes: (1) a pedagogic one for the insider, that he may see more vividly, and more fully enter into, the essentials of the Christian Faith lying beyond the nonessentials and recognize how fruitful or distorting the various nonessentials may be in the communication of the essentials; and (2) an apologetic one for the outsider, that, in a measure freed of the burden of implausible and incomprehensible concepts, of propositions and images, the essentials restated may appear more plausible to him, with the hope that through the grace of God he may more readily come to faith therein.

For a year or two during my youth in Southern California I sought to earn spending money by selling the *Saturday Evening Post.* Part of the package deal was the requirement that I sell a proportionate number of copies of the *Ladies' Home Journal* and of

Country Gentleman. As I recall it, I did not have too much trouble with the woman's magazine; but I found it exceedingly difficult to market the rural-oriented man's publication on the streets of Hollywood. Whatever may have been the wisdom of the company's policy generally, as its local salesman I was simply burdened with too big a package; I finally gave up the enterprise. Likewise overburdened have been clergy and laity who are seeking to "sell" the Faith; and many of them have become similarly discouraged.

Whether or not this particular effort will serve the intended apologetic purpose, I have had some experience of the possibility. As a result of the previous "heresy" controversy in which I was unwittingly involved (and during which I received more negative mail than letters of commendation), there is no evidence that a single one of the faithful actually left the Church because of my stated positions or because of the fact that I was not officially condemned by my Church for them. Rather, I have learned directly, and through other clergy, of a good many people who turned toward the Church when they learned that certain beliefs which they thought the Church held to be essential could be left as open questions. Even in the short time since the publication of *Honest to God,* I have heard of a good number of instances where it has had the same effect on readers.[4] (Similarly, there is no evidence that anyone has been driven out of the Church by the fact of its publication or by the fact that its episcopal author still remains a bishop of the Church.)

To return to the first purpose mentioned above, there are many people within the fold who have not really grasped the heart of the Christian message because they are bogged down by too many doctrines, mores, precepts, customs, symbols and other traditions, with no sense of differentiation between the relative essentiality and nonessentiality of the respective items. For such Christians, the Faith has an air of unreality and they have become rather numb to the whole thing. Many of these are loyal enough—or indifferent

---

[4] See also some of the letters from readers of the book, collected in the work cited in n. 2 above.

enough—to be willing to take the whole thing "on faith," but as a result do not see the forest for the trees. Clearly stated and sound efforts at theological reconstruction can bring them closer to the heart of the matter. However successful this volume may be to this end, many of us are convinced that theological reconstruction can bring more reality, conviction, and consequent action, enabling many more Churchmen to be more effective witnesses to Christ and His Church in the world.

It is clear from the very fact that others have put things differently in times past and present, that no absoluteness can be claimed for any one effort at reconstruction: the most that can be claimed for it is that it is *a* way of thinking about and presenting the Christian Faith. Others, with equal purity of heart and soundness of mind, will disagree with particular analyses. And there are still others who prefer a wholly different way of getting at the subject. It is on this deeper level of basic approach that the important contrasts emerge.

At bottom, there are two basic methodologies in the realm of philosophical and religious thinking, and the difference between them is the source of most surface disagreements about specific theological and ethical questions. There are those whose system is primarily *ontological* and there are those whose system is primarily *existential*. The ontologist pictures reality in terms of a hierarchy of absolute categories all logically linked together. The existentialist knows of no such structure of ontological reality and either regards all things as relative rather than absolute, as particular rather than generic or universal (this is the case with the secularist existentialist), or accepts only one Reality as absolute and regards all else as relative and particular. In this the Christian existentialist is ontological in the sense that he believes in one *"On"* as absolute and invariable: the Ultimate Ground of all being, revealed as over-all Claimant and Redeemer with whose life we are conjoined through the remembrance of His mighty acts. While the Christian existentialist would concur with the ontologists as to the necessity of having "earthen vessels" for "this treasure," he would insist that the treasure alone, and none of the vessels, is ultimate. In the field of theology, he too will indulge in doctrinal statements; but he will not regard his attempt at this worthy enterprise as final any more than he would regard others' attempts as final. In the field of ethics, ontologists generally assert the unchangeable reality of natural law or of commandments of universal application. The Christian existentialist will recognize the absolute character of the over-all claim represented by the First Great Commandment (all-embracing love of God) and the pragmatic value of moral codes; but in the last analysis he will affirm a "situational ethic": that is, an ethical judgment or action must always reflect the special requirements of the concrete living context in which it takes place. In the fields of ecclesiastical government and worship, the ontologist will tend to see certain forms as an unalterable part of the package; the existentialist, while valuing structures and forms, will attribute to them no other than a relative place in the scheme of things.

It is on this level that sooner or later the really significant open debate will ensue. On what grounds will this issue of basic methodology be resolved by a given individual? The proof of the validity of one system or the other? No. When we are dealing with meaning, first premises can never be proved: they are taken on faith, and this applies to basic methodology as fully as it applies to the Object of belief itself. Different temperaments and personality-patterns surely enter here, and certainly upbringing and education—theological or otherwise—have a bearing on how a given individual will do his thinking or rethinking. To the degree that he is free of these conditioning factors, a person confronted or reconfronted with the choice should ask the question as to which methodology is the most *plausible* (as is pointed out in Chapter I, plausibility is the most significant factor in deciding what one should put one's faith in). Under the test of plausibility the existentialist has on his side considerable empirical weight. When one applies *Historismus* (the approach called "the history of ideas," a methodology employed in other disciplines) to the categories of doctrinal formulation, ethical rules, ecclesiastical structures, and modes of worship, the nonabsolute character of the items in these categories would seem to be manifest, as we shall see in Chapters II through IV on earthen vessels, dealing respectively with "creed," "code," and "cult."[5]

My readers who think in thoroughgoing ontological categories, while perhaps conceding that I do "believe," will feel that I believe in far too little. There are many things in which the ontologist believes which I do not believe in the sense of accepting them as ultimate. Yet many of these I, nevertheless, *accept*—but only as instrumental to that which it is hoped, through positive affirmations and through deflation of what seems to me nonessential, emerges "loud and clear": namely, the Gospel—with a relevant view of God, a "high" Christology, a maximum claim in ethics, and the centrality of Baptism and the Eucharist in the life of the Church. Thus this book is at one with even the most conventional theologians in these essential things of the Catholic Faith, "the faith once and for all delivered to the Saints." I am grateful for this fellowship in the Gospel with those who find more appealing the ontological methodology—in the spirit of the words of the Holy Apostle, "But what matter, I or they? This is what we all proclaim, and this is what you believed." (I COR. 15:11, NEB)

✠ JAMES A. PIKE

The Cathedral Close, San Francisco
Feast of the Conversion of St. Paul, 1964

---

[5] In this connection, while this book is written out of Christian, rather than merely Anglican, concern, a good number of the examples are drawn from my own tradition because (a) I am more familiar with it, (b) we have a particularly interesting collection of earthen vessels, and (c) it is more seemly that a critique by an Episcopalian be more obviously directed to his own Church than to others.

I: WHY BELIEVE?

ALL TOO many people are diffident about the discussion of any particular belief, and therefore of all beliefs, because they see no point in believing at all. This is different from the attitude of those who affirm that we cannot know anything religiously. The diffidence is more fundamental. If asked to spell it out, one of these *diffidenti* might say, "Maybe all you say is true. Maybe it's a truth that can be known. Maybe some people need religion; I'm glad for them to have it. As for me, I don't need it, and I'm not interested in it. My life is full enough with the things I am interested in: my work, my chosen forms of recreation, art and music, and my circle of friends. I don't see any necessity for religious belief. If it means something to you, fine; it doesn't to me."

What does one say to that? Those who think and speak thus are often nice, congenial, and decent people, reasonably well adjusted, fairly good to their family and neighbors, and sometimes concerned for constructive causes. So in many instances it would appear that, looked at from the outside, such religious *diffidenti* actually do not need anything more.

What we are dealing with here is not an isolated view of a small, esoteric group in our society. Of those not actively involved in a Church a majority actually hold such a position. Convinced atheism is much rarer; rarer too is a conscious agnosticism. The latter two positions represent some real thought at one time of life or another—or perhaps consistently—about religious questions. For a much larger group their reaction to all religious questions is simply, "I couldn't care less."

Before proceeding to answer the question "Why believe?" it is well to be realistic about the chances of convincing the *diffidenti* by logic and arguments—no matter how sound. Often behind this calm attitude of indifference are specific factors in the personal histories of individuals which have set up blocks to current religious interest. For example, if the diffident grew up in Church, the block may be that in his unconscious mind he associates with the compulsory churchgoing of his childhood the authority figure behind that compulsion, namely, his father; and maybe, consciously or unconsciously, he really hates his father. The connection with the father-figure in reaction to God has been a long-standing theme of psychiatry. Well known is the view of secular psychiatrists, beginning with Freud, that the figure of God is a projection, from the unconscious, of father-attachment. Somewhat less known is the equally relevant view of religiously oriented psychiatrists that the rejection of God can be the projection, from the unconscious, of father-hatred.

Or perhaps, not liking the denomination in which he was raised, he may have overgeneralized and concluded, "The Church is not for me." This is not merely complacent disinterest; there is a feeling-tone in it. His transition is not merely an intellectual one; there is both joy and pain in his "release." Something permanent has happened to his make-up. Therefore, the mere intellectual presentation of a "case" would doubtless leave him still uninvolved.

Or he may lately have been behaving in a way which is in conflict with his moral upbringing. Since his religious tradition does not endorse his new mode of life, he finds religion somewhat inconvenient to have on his mind.

On the other hand, the diffident may have been raised in a household in which there was not the least interest in the Church except for "sprinkling" occasions: water at birth, rice at marriage, and dirt at death. He may never have seen the inside of a Sunday school or glanced at the Bible. He has not been through a pattern of rejection, or through any turmoil with regard to religion. His diffidence is about like that of most people toward vegetarianism; it's nothing he'd ever been involved in or particularly thought about.

The point of this analysis is simply that what is to follow in the way of an answer can be communicated with varying degrees of effectiveness, depending upon the particular blocks of the people concerned. (Also it is meant as a warning to one eager to communicate the faith that he should not be disappointed if somehow his best logic does not seem to get across). In the case of those who were raised in a Church and left it, a "break-through" is possible if some great personal grief or ennui or despair moves in like a tidal wave to a point where the particular block is reduced. Those in the last category, who have never known religion, are the more susceptible to an objective approach.

Yet the fact is that *everybody believes, everybody has a religion.* The truth of this statement depends on an understanding of what "belief" and "religion" mean. They actually mean the same thing except that semantically we use the words on different levels: Belief is applicable to the trust we have that the storekeeper will return our change; religion starts on a somewhat more cosmic level. Both have to do with the basic assumptions on which we operate in our daily reliances and decision-making. Everybody has such assumptions, and here are some of them: (1) there is an external world corresponding to the pictures in our heads; (2) living is worthwhile; (3) truth has a value greater than falsehood; (4) some things are more valuable than others: e.g., being at the bedside of one's dying mother is more important than being at a cocktail party.

In all this we come down to a scale of priorities. In this regard, every man has a god or gods. That last double reference is not insignificant.

Some people have just *one* god—one thing that is of the very utmost importance to them and one thing that determines decision-making. For some, it is a god traditionally known as Mammon. Their instinctive reaction to any question is, "What's in it for me?" "Does it pay off?" This may govern their choice of social engagements. It may determine with whom they agree to have lunch, which letters they acknowledge and which they ignore. There can be a certain *integration* in such an approach. Such a person can act in a unified and integrated way because he has one clear focus. This is possible, too, with other gods: Baal, Venus, Apollo, Mars (though the individual worshiper of each might well be surprised to know what his god is). Generally, at some point in life, monolatry of this sort breaks down, because no one of such gods is adequate—each has feet of clay; no one covers the whole field with all that life is and all the potential responsiveness that there is in man. But before that time, the worship of such a god can impart direction, order, and consistency to life.

Most people, however, are polytheists. They are under claim from various of these gods: no one single thing dominates, and their lives are torn. When there is, for example, a conflict between making money or making love, or between prestige and principle, they undergo a great strain and much of their life is inconsistent. If the situation is difficult enough, they may become schizoid, if not schizophrenic. One who worships the many, is many.

But far be it from the Christian to claim that polytheism is not religious. It is important for the Christian to keep in mind that whichever of the two alternatives—monotheism or polytheism—is significant in the life of any one person, he is nevertheless religious. Consciously or unconsciously, he *believes*. He acts daily with trust in certain presuppositions and assumptions. As to the value of the goals and the aims which he is following, he does not act upon proof, but upon belief.

At this point, we should be modest about the claims of Christianity. We certainly do not claim that the existence of God can be proved; and we cannot claim that our value-pattern can be established by logic. All we can claim is that we who are Christians believe what we do, and seek to live it out, on the basis of a known and *chosen* perspective and priority scale, whereas the *diffidenti*, while operating likewise on the basis of a given perspective and a value-pattern, do so unconsciously without thoughtful evaluation of the perspective and the priority scale. We can claim further that a *careful* examination of these various secular values, as compared with a careful examination of the Christian position, may well show that the latter is the more adequate, the more unifying, and covers more of the whole of life's experience.

Thus, the answer to "Why believe?" is that everyone believes anyway. It is valuable for each person to *know* what he really believes, to know on what premise he really operates as he makes his decisions, as he loves and hates, as he works and plays.

What, then, is belief? This question should be considered further before turning to any particular article of belief and the soundness thereof, for many people who would like to believe in the Christian Faith are unable to do so, largely because they start from a false conception of what belief really comes down to.

First, some of the things that belief is *not*.

1. In our scientific age, there are many who claim that they accept only things which can be demonstrated. Such a one knows what the melting point of a particular metal is because, in identical tests conducted many times in the laboratory, samples of this particular metal have melted at that particular temperature. He cannot find the nature and attributes of God—or find God at all—in the same manner; hence he does not see how he can believe. The syllogism is, in effect:

All that can be believed is that which can be demonstrated by methods like those appropriate to the laboratory sciences;
The articles of the Christian Faith cannot be so established;
Therefore, the articles of the Christian Faith cannot be believed.

The minor premise can be conceded outright. From time to time attempts have been made by well-meaning Christians (some of them scientists themselves) to prove that Christianity is scientific—indeed, to adduce scientific evidence in support of given doctrines. (A rather far-fetched example is the use of partheno-genesis among tsetse flies in Africa as support for believe in the Virgin Birth.) Actually, this is a vain hope; in fact, even if we supposed for a moment that such efforts were sound, the result would not be faith, as we shall see later.

In other words, a person for whom the scientific method is dominant will much more likely come to belief if he does not *expect* it to be supported by conclusive laboratory evidence. Though the minor premise of his syllogism is totally correct, the major premise is totally incorrect; hence the conclusion does not hold.

2. Somewhat related is the position of those who are of a philosophic bent; who recognize that in religion one is dealing with things intangible; who do not expect anything like laboratory proof; but who nevertheless expect firm, *logical* proof. This expectancy does have a place—albeit a limited one—in the texture of believing. But that we cannot prove religious truth by formal logic can be shown easily with reference to the fundamental Reality of the Judeo-Christian tradition, namely, God. We can use the syllogistic method from some basic *given*, but in this case God is the basic Given. If He is at the end of a sound syllogism instead of at the start of it, then He is not God; He is a corollary to some more basic reality or truth. And this is a contradiction in terms. If I say "X, therefore 'God,'" then "X" is more ultimate than the god I end up with in the reasoning.

3. A less reflective type of person may not be waiting for scientific or logical proof, but may just not feel he "has faith." By this he means he is not grasped by a feeling: he is waiting for *emotional* proof. Now emotion is sometimes associated with faith; some-times believing people do have certain feelings about their relation-ship to God—feelings describable and indescribable. Whether there is emotion, and what its extent may be, depend upon the varying temperaments of individuals and upon the circumstances. But the emotion is not the faith, nor is it a prerequisite thereto.

These three examples, different as they are, have one thing in common: an unnecessary "handicap" has been added. Believing in the Christian Faith is not easy; but there is no use making it any harder than it is.

Now that we have considered what belief is not, we return to what it is. It is essentially *trust*, by an act of will. In this field, more than any other, analogies are imperfect; but it is something like deciding to get married. Of course, there is some emotion connected with a decision to marry; if there were not, it would in any case be a bad decision. But the question is not simply one of feeling an emotion to a sufficient degree of intensity. Nor is the answer to be found in scientific proof or philosophical logic. But this does not mean that there is nothing to go on: the decision to get married is an act of will, based on certain plausible inferences drawn from experience, regarding the reliability, character, and values of the prospective mate. Moreover, the mate is a source, if not *the* source, of the response. Likewise with faith in God. The process of arriving at belief does not simply operate within the putative believer. When one has gone past the line into faith, he believes that God is the *Source* of his faith.

Assume the seeker is looking for the Ultimate. Certainly he cannot start his reasoning from a *more* ultimate basis than that which he is seeking. Therefore, his finding (or being found by) the Ultimate will have to be by some other means than empirical proof or sheer reason. Axioms precede theorems (for those who remember geometry), and axioms are not proved.

But axioms are not necessarily antirational. Sound axioms make sense in that they are in accord with customary experience. As Søren Kierkegaard has reminded us, in religion there must be a "leap of faith." But one does not leap toward just *anything*. Otherwise astrology, Rosicrucianism, "snake-handling," and the Judeo-Christian tradition would all have equal claims. A sensible person will only leap toward a footing that appears to be fairly solid. How does one decide what is fairly solid? Here reason, dethroned earlier in our argument, re-enters. We cannot establish the Christian Faith by reasoning; but reasoning (including syllogisms) can help to point toward the most plausible of the alternatives.

Here I can speak from experience. I was raised in a religious tradition which claimed to be able through scholastic philosophy, based primarily on St. Thomas Aquinas (and through him, on Aristotle), to be able to *prove* the existence of God and certain other basic premises of Christianity. In reopening this whole question after some intervening years of agnosticism, while I remained unconvinced that this proof was possible, I did find that a number of the same arguments effectively pointed toward the *plausibility* of the basic elements of the Christian Faith. All in all, I found Christianity the most plausible perspective on reality and hence acted in faith—by an act of the will—to commit myself to be a Christian again.

But in the end, the latter decision was an *act of the will.*

The point is made (though perhaps subtly for most people) by the wording of the opening phrase of the Apostles' Creed: We do not affirm in church that we "believe that there is a God," rather we affirm, "I believe in God." When a man says, "I believe in my wife," he is saying something different from "I believe that I have a wife." The latter is a verifiable fact, whether he is at home or away on a trip (thanks to the good offices of the telephone system). His first statement represents an act of faith. He is saying that he puts his trust in her, he has cast his lot with her. So when a man says, "I believe in God," he is saying, "I have bet my life on Him."

This does not necessarily mean that he has a great emotional feeling about it. In affirming that he believes in his wife, a man may have an emotional feeling or simply a quiet, confident trust. The same with God.

Is that all there is? Is there no verification at any point? Yes, there is. Just as one who wisely takes a leap of faith into marriage may well find afterward that his faith was justified by the actual day-to-day living relationship, so too for one who takes the leap of faith of belief in God—if it is a real commitment. And here is where the empirical method re-enters. Day by day (perhaps many times each day) he will find facts which "verify" the initial trust. When I did this in my adult life, I found that rapidly I was understanding my past better (why this particular plan didn't work out, why this person liked me and this one didn't, why I was unhappy at this point and happy at the other); I found that I had a better basis for focusing on my future and making decisions; I understood people better as I went along—and understood myself better as well. Thus from what was sheer faith and trust, I began to come to a sort of verified *knowledge.*

Thus in the implication above that the method of coming to faith was unlike that of laboratory science, the case was somewhat overstated. There is a genuine analogy between the two. What does a research scientist do when he gets an idea about what might be true? He does not take any old hypothesis into the laboratory for exhaustive experimentation. First, he analyzes the matter to see if the possible conclusion to be drawn is plausible, is congruent with other verified data and conclusions; and by a sort of common sense he intuits whether or not the possible conclusion would make sense. Then he goes into the laboratory and tests. If after a sufficiently objective testing, the hypothesis "pans out," he then feels that he *knows.* Similarly, the seeker after a religious perspective pauses to analyze the plausibility and the congruence of the Christian outlook on reality. Then he takes it into the "laboratory": in this case the laboratory is his own life. Having committed himself, if he then finds that his life makes better sense (past, present, and future), he *knows.*

All this is said and affirmed in the creed by the phrase, "I believe."

Assume that this leap of faith has been taken. This is not a theoretical assumption, because it happens to people every day. What is its consequence?

In answer, it might be worthwhile to outline a few things that happen to the research scientist as a result of the process which we have used as analogy:

1. His knowledge pattern is not the same any more. It has expanded. This will have a bearing on his future decisions and on particular questions that come up from time to time. The truth is bigger—or different (perhaps his research has debunked a false assumption he had held for years) from what it was before. Thus the whole matter bears on his future decision-making, his future scientific judgment.

2. He will almost inevitably *share* his findings. In fact, he may write a learned article in order to share his conclusions with his colleagues.

3. He will be moved to explore further the implications of his new-found conviction. This effort will relate both to the level of theory and to the level of experience.

When an adult "joins the Church," if nothing happens about his life, about his habits, or about his conversation, then obviously his *real* faith has not changed. He has simply done something formally and ecclesiastically. But if he has gone through the process seriously, then his life will be different.

In the first century of the Christian era, a group of people went through this process and were grasped by a great Faith. As a result the whole course of Western civilization was changed (though perhaps not as radically as some of us assume—it was predicted by a contemporary pagan that the Christians would "overturn the world"; we really haven't). But nevertheless tremendous things have happened because of this original impetus, an impetus which keeps being revived—with new things happening.

Jesus said, "By their fruits, ye shall know them." He said in another place, "Not everyone that saith unto me, Lord, Lord, shall enter into the kingdom of heaven; but he that doeth the will of my Father." While the results are not the *reason* for the changed conviction, if results do not come, one can wonder whether in fact there has been a change. The truth is not enough. The unknown author of the Fourth Gospel reminds us that we should *do* the truth. The consequence of belief is action.

Misunderstanding of the nature of faith is not the only obstacle to acceptance of Christianity. Some years ago a fellow priest and I wrote a book called *Roadblocks to Faith*.[1] In the form of a dialogue between a skeptic and a believer we there sought to deal with some of the most familiar ways resistance to Christian belief is articulated. These roadblocks are:

Isn't religion unscientific?
Which is the true religion?
Isn't ethics enough?
Doesn't evil disprove God?
I have my own religion.

In the case of each of these objections the difficulty was principally ignorance of, or misunderstanding of, the authentic Christian position. Our effort in that book was to clarify for the outsider his misconceptions of what the Church affirms.

But there is an even more formidable roadblock to the understanding and acceptance of Christianity and it is one which, by and large, spokesmen for the Church have themselves erected. It works not only to keep people out; it keeps insiders really outsiders—as far as the real thing goes. And it tends to keep Christianity irrelevant.

What is this roadblock? It is hard to discern, harder to state: but in the end it is churchmen's well-intentioned *idolatry*. What is historically conditioned is presented as eternal, what is relative is presented as absolute, what is "packaging" is presented as the product, what are mores is presented as morals, what is fallible is presented as infallible, what is contingent is presented as ultimate, what is secondary is presented as primary, what is nonessential is presented as essential, what is custom and "machinery" is presented as final reality; the notions of men are presented as the mind of God, the words of men are presented as the will of God.

Different Churches and different spokesmen do this in differing

[1] With the Very Rev. John M. Krumm (New York: Morehouse-Gorham, 1954; Collier Books, 1963).

ways and to different degrees. But in almost every Church what the outsider confronts is a complex series of doctrinal propositions, an extensive set of do's and don'ts, an elaborate structure of government and relationships, a thick holy book of diverse materials with varying degrees of clarity and obfuscation, and in some Churches a complicated scheme of public worship.

That every interested seeker is not about to buy the whole package is not surprising. Rather, what is surprising is that so many do, or seem to. But when they *do*, without discrimination, they simply add to the number who have finalized the unfinal, who are buttresses to ecclesiastical rigidity, who become denominational guardians, who join in the cry of "heresy" when relative and non-essential things are questioned, who resist reform and renewal. Many "join the Church" knowing little—and caring little—about these refinements, feeling that the institution is generally good and helpful, but missing the challenge and the power at the heart of the matter.

As we shall see, there is a legitimate role for most of these relative and secondary aspects of religion; it is their worship as absolutes that is the roadblock. And more than this, such religious absolutism is actually irreligious: it is blasphemy. There is only *one* Ultimate: God as known and experienced in His over-all claim, His mighty acts. To make anything else ultimate is idolatry. *Anything* else: whether a particular doctrinal formulation, a particular book or books, a particular scheme of church government, a particular office or person, a particular ethical rule, a particular way of worship. None of these is an essential of the Gospel. And it is the Gospel we are to commend to others.

Hence, before we seek to state what the Gospel *is*, it is necessary to state what it is not—though has been presumed to be. This task of pruning is the burden of the following three chapters, utilizing the categories often thought to be the essentials of religion: the three C's—Creed, Code, and Cult.

II: CREED

Not content to reserve ultimacy to God and His mighty acts, many Christians attribute finality to men's words *about* Him, His claim, His saving power. For many the final authority is the literal text of the Holy Bible; for many it is the words of Creeds and the decrees of Councils of the Church; for many it is the *ex cathedra* pronouncement of a particular prelate; for many it is the words of a denominational confession of faith. The selected medium judges *all else*; there is no looking beyond it for judgment of *it*. The object of these attachments is to secure certainty in religion; but as is the case in every idolatry, they are not entirely successful toward this end. As we consider these various ways of finalizing less than the Ultimate, we shall see that they lack consistency and generally fail in both relevance and communication.

Let us turn first to bibliolatry. The fundamentalist claims to accept unquestioningly the words of the Holy Bible—and all of them. He feels threatened if any particular assertion or narrative in the Scriptures is challenged, qualified, or treated as myth. His usual retort to any such attempt is, "If you don't believe it all, then why believe any of it?" (Paradoxically enough, this is often the retort of the secularist to the Christian who exercises discrimination as to what he accepts literally in the Bible; here the

unbeliever displays an all-or-nothing fundamentalism in reverse.)
The fundamentalist fears that the whole house will fall if the
plumbing is modernized or if the porch is renovated. Any attempt
to rethink and restate the verities to which the Bible witnesses he
suspects of infidelity and unbelief. Sometimes the bibliolatrist
focuses upon an even lesser god, namely, a particular translation;
such was the lady who said, "If the King James Version was good
enough for Saint Paul, it is good enough for me!" The panic of
these devotees at the suggestion that such a god might have feet of
clay can result in an almost incredible fanaticism, e.g., the charge
of certain extreme fundamentalists that the Revised Standard
Version is somehow part of a Communist plot. Yet, so obviously
a "mixed bag" as the Scriptures cannot be accepted consistently
even by those professing so to do. By and large, the details of
conduct and of worship as supplied in the Pentateuch are ignored;
yet there is willingness to use particular proof-texts from this
material to buttress any present attitude or commitment.

An interesting example is the use by the Roman Catholic
Church of God's punishment of Onan by death as support for its
strictures against certain methods of birth control. The mores of
Onan's time (like those of some tribes today) required levirate
marriage: it was a man's obligation to take to him the wife of a
childless deceased brother in order to produce offspring and thus
eternal life for the brother. Onan did indeed take to him his
deceased brother's wife, but avoided conception by the practice of
coitus interruptus. The passage which had exalted this portion of
the mores into morals also described the sanction: Onan was struck
dead by God on the spot (Gen. 38:8-10). This narrative had early
been used by the Roman Catholic moral theologians as proof of
the sin of masturbation, called then by the title "Onanism." But in
the later apologetics on birth control[1] it has been used as proof of
the sinfulness of the deliberate avoidance of conception by "un-
natural" means. Actually, however, as the text and context make

[1] See more fully Chap. III.

clear, the offense was not the *means* but the *end:* the implementation of Onan's unwillingness to father a child for the sake of his brother. But this levirate requirement the Roman Catholic Church has by no means consistently supported. As a matter of fact, in the time of Henry VIII the canon law on this point was exactly the opposite, i.e., a man might *not* marry his deceased brother's wife; and the fact that the king had done precisely this (albeit with a papal dispensation) was the basis of his application for the annulment[2] of his marriage to Katherine of Aragon.

To move to the other end of the ecclesiastical spectrum, Protestant fundamentalists almost never practice the Unction of the Sick, although this is explicitly called for in the Epistle of James.[3] And as for the prophetic books of the Bible, diffidence among fundamentalists about historical context, textual criticism, and dating renders most of the passages meaningless on their face, requiring the importation of meanings from the believer's head: "eisegesis" rather than exegesis. And such preoccupation with the literal hides the depth meaning in a mythological narrative and dims its relevance for today. This is particularly evident in the case of the Edenic myth. Taking the narrative as literal history results in an absurd and incredible explanation of man's problem of getting right with God: the punishment of each individual in the human race because two members of the race violated an arbitrary fiat of their Maker by eating an apple. As to such a "God" who could so behave, a person reasonably intelligent and ethically sensitive would be forced to be an atheist. But released from historicism, the narrative portrays in perennial terms the conflict in every man—today as of yesteryear.[4]

For the rigid fundamentalist, "having everything in writing" seems to avoid the necessity of the leap of faith. Explicit texts in the Bible are used to prove God, Jesus Christ, and so forth. In the words of the familiar evangelistic hymn,

[2] Not divorce in the modern sense; there was then no such thing in Western Christendom.

[3] Jas. 5:14-15; see more fully App. B, p. 149.

[4] See pp. 96-97.

Jesus loves me, this I know,
For the Bible tells me so.

But what proves the Bible? This anthology of essays, monographs, and brochures was selected from the works of many authors and editors—in the case of the Old Testament by the rabbis in exile at Jamnia after the fall of Jerusalem in A.D. 71, and in the case of the New by the Church Fathers in the fourth century. The Bible is not self-evidently final or self-authenticating. Nonfundamentalists accept various portions with varying degrees of seriousness, to the extent that each portion accords with faith in God, His total claim, His mighty acts.

The Scriptures as a whole have so high a priority because they are the literature of a people, that is, the Old and New Israel, who were in general seeking to respond to God's claim and His redemptive activity. When the Bible is accepted in this way it is evident that there already has been a leap of faith—in such a God. What is not as easily perceived is the fact that the prior acceptance of the Bible as ultimate and its subsequent use to prove certain things about God and His activity is also a leap of faith—absolute faith in this thick book of words. But if faith in the Scriptures is absolute, the faith is in something less than God. If a "God" is derived as a corollary to that faith then the derivative is not God: it is an idol.

In answer to the Protestant fundamentalist, the Catholic churchman (whether Roman or Anglican, or other) asserts, quite reasonably, that the Church is prior to the Bible. Abraham, whom in archetypal or literal terms he regards as the founder of the Church, did not possess a copy of the Pentateuch; he is written up in it! But he had the Faith, and was in covenant with the living God. St. Paul did not have pocket testaments available to distribute as he went about the Mediterranean; yet are we to say that he was not a Christian? The books of the Bible were written and edited *by* churchmen (of the old and new Israel) and it was the Church (again, old and new), through representative groups of churchmen, that selected the books which form the Holy Scriptures.

This answer is a good antidote to bibliolatry; but often it becomes at the same time the first premise of an *ecclesiolatry:* The Bible is not final, it is the Church's book; but the Church is final. What is to be believed about God, Jesus, eternal life, conduct, and so forth? What "the Church teaches" about these various things. Against the Protestant principle of private interpretation is the view that the Church is the only legitimate interpreter of the Scriptures. Yet since even a cursory knowledge of the history of doctrine indicates that different parts of the Christian Church have taught different things at different times, this Church-centered absolutism has of necessity to be narrowed, that an answer may be given to the questions: What Church? What statements of the Church? Some denominations are direct and clear on these points. For the Roman Catholic Church, absolute and beyond reform are the doctrinal statements of the Councils that received, or are believed to have received, Papal approval, plus the *ex cathedra* pronouncements of the Pope apart from a Council.[5] The doctrines thus proclaimed are all equally absolute and all are alike in claiming that belief in each is essential to salvation, whether the doctrines touch the divinity of Christ or the 1954 dogma of the Assumption of Mary into heaven.

To the degree that they are true to their formative principles, Churches of the Lutheran and of the Reformed-Presbyterian traditions have exalted as final their respective confessions of faith, such as the Augsburg, Heidelberg, and Westminster Confessions. Each of these, for its respective tradition, is—in theory at least—the absolute judge of orthodoxy; and nothing judges the Confession. As to the Confessions there is increasingly a critical spirit—which is a joy to some and a horror to others. But for the orthodox in the given tradition, a particular Confession of Faith has the

[5] It would appear that the Fall, 1964, session of Vatican Council II may qualify this position.

answer to the questions: What Church? and What pronouncements of that Church? Thus, Who and What is God? He is
Who and What the Confession says He is, and so forth—throughout the whole range of doctrine.[6] (Some "Confessional Churches"
have by now officially deabsolutized their Confessions.)

Some Anglicans, particularly of the more evangelical persuasion,
have tried to erect the jejune Articles of Religion into a Confession; but Anglicans as a whole have never been very confessional
by disposition. Except for the forensic use of an Article now and
again as a weapon—proof-text fashion—generally the Articles are
simply regarded as the allergic reaction of the Anglican Church,
in a particularly trying period, to the fact of "Papists" on the one
side and Puritans on the other (though its *ad hoc* retorts are for
the most part quite commendable, in the light of the historical
context, on the particular points to which they are addressed).
Other Anglicans finalize "the teaching of the undivided Church,"
undaunted by the fact that a single Church has rarely existed in
history. Assuming "the undivided Church" to refer to a reality
(namely, the position of the majority of the bishops in the Councils of the Church before the schism between the East and West),
they regard the pronouncements of these Councils (there is some
division in the ranks as to how many of the Councils are infallible)
as absolute.[7]

But for some, principally of the Anglo-Catholic persuasion,
decrees of the Councils (which principally dealt with Christology)
do not present a large enough platform of finalities. Certain other
essentials of Catholic doctrine are arrived at by the use of what is

[6] Apparently at least one of the Reformed Churches in South Africa has an
additional item of finality: cf. the recent unfrocking of a clergyman-professor
for teaching contrary to *apartheid*, for which the Reformed Churches in that
country supply biblical and theological apologetic.

[7] Actually such a view of things is contradicted by Article XXI on the
Councils: ". . . And when they be gathered together, (forasmuch as they
be an assembly of men, whereof all be not governed with the Spirit and
Word of God,) they may err, and sometimes have erred, even in things per-
taining unto God." (Notice how readily, even after the comments on the
Articles just above, the author turns to the Articles for a proof-text. In this,
at least, he is very Anglican!)

called the Canon of St. Vincent of Lerins: *Quod semper, quod ubique, quod ab omnibus*. If indeed there has been anything which has been accepted "always, everywhere and by everyone," this would be an ecclesiastical form of the political maxim *Vox populi, vox dei*: in short, if everybody thinks so, it's so. Incidentally, throughout the centuries of the alleged undivided Church everybody thought that the earth was flat, and that heaven was above and hell beneath. For very few proponents of the Vincentian Canon is such a cosmology today beyond question.

Other Anglicans are content with a narrower platform of finality: the historic Creeds. Many who take this stance would themselves be put off by the Athanasian Creed, with its anathemas and its intricate web of abstract concepts. (They say that some English vicars like to have the curate preach on Trinity Sunday, while the vicar sits at his prayer desk checking off in the Athanasian Creed the young assistant's heresies!) Most American Episcopalians have never seen the Athanasian Creed, since it was deliberately excluded from the American Prayer Book (the Nicene Creed barely made it); hence we can assume that most of those who speak of the Creeds as final mean the Apostles' and Nicene Creeds. These are not biblical fundamentalists; they are creedal fundamentalists.[8]

Virtually all creedal affirmations through history have been specific *ad hoc* reactions to the position of some prominent heretic (or supposed heretic) whose views had commended themselves to a minority (or, as in the case of Arianism, perhaps a majority) of the flock, or to a schismatic Church. For example, in his well-intentioned attempt to answer our Lord's question, "Who do you say that I am?" Arius used a compound word based on the current

[8] Actually the phrase cannot be limited to them alone; all the forms of absolutism we are discussing are creedal. For the Protestant fundamentalist the Bible is his Creed; for the truly Confessional churchman the given Confession of Faith is his Creed; for the Roman Catholic certain conciliar decrees and papal utterances together form his full Creed (indeed, the most detailed and normative Roman Catholic Confession of Faith bears the name, "The Creed of Pius IV").

Greek philosophical system, *homoiousion:* Jesus Christ is "of like substance" with the Father. Aware of how destructive such a view would be to the core of the Faith, the majority of the Fathers in council answered by dropping one *iota* and affirming that He is *homoousion,* "of the same substance" with the Father. This was the thing to say, and at the time it was the way to say it. In forensics, communication is generally best achieved by answering a question in the terms in which it is asked. But through the quite worthy and understandable desire to provide a defense which would lock out all future Arii, this answer was made a part of a permanent statement of the Faith. So, what began as a rebuttal meant to say what the Faith *is not* has ever after been used as a vehicle of proclaiming what the Faith *is*. What is generally overlooked is that if Arius had stated his position in different terms, the reply would have been set forth in a different word or words. And while all this was a dialogue *about* the Ultimate, by many the selected term is now itself viewed as ultimate.

The fact is that this word (and the concept behind it), or any other, is of human devising and part of the changing scene. Fashions in philosophy change as they do in women's clothing (though perhaps not as rapidly). What is involved is not merely semantics—the change in the meaning of words; what is involved is a change in conceptual structure—in the shape, size, and relative location of the pigeonholes used by men to sort out their impressions of reality. The idea of substance is one such pigeonhole in one such filing system. All pigeonholes and filing systems are temporal, historically conditioned, and finite. Even at the same time such a word as *homoousion* was first used officially, it was inadequate: man's mind is never up to grasping and labeling the ultimate verities. As the centuries have rolled on, the word has become less and less adequate—indeed finally irrelevant and virtually a cipher as far as communication is concerned. Churchmen in the meanwhile have, in this regard as in other regards, exalted the temporal as the eternal, the contingent as the final, the *ad hoc* as the universal, the finite as the infinite. Overlooked is the

Apostle's reminder that "we have this treasure in earthen vessels." For the "orthodox" churchman all too often the vessel has become the treasure. For many thoughtful men in later ages, the vessel has been viewed as a museum piece—either attractive or unattractive, but not effective as an active carrier of truth and reality.

A quaint but illuminating example of the time-bound character of declarations thought to be perennial, where the character of the answer arose out of the semantics and conceptuality of a particular challenge and was a response in kind, is the so-called "black rubric" at the end of the Communion Office in the Second Prayer Book of Edward VI. This Prayer Book by rubrical direction continued kneeling for the reception of Holy Communion; but the compiler, Archbishop Cranmer, was aware of the theological sensitivities of those who were eager to avoid any implication of either adoration of the sacramental bread or wine or the affirmation of the presence in the elements of the natural flesh and blood of Christ. Hence the rubric, while seeking to justify the continuance of the custom of kneeling to receive Communion on both pious and practical grounds, takes pains to deny that "any adoration is done, or ought to be done, either of the sacramental bread or wine there bodily received, or to any real and essential presence there being of Christ's natural flesh and blood." After asserting that such adoration would be idolatry, as against the positions of transubstantiationists and consubstantiationists (each of whom seem to affirm that Christ's natural body is in fact present in the elements), the answer is given in terms of the same cosmology used by these contenders—a cosmology which assumes a three-layer universe, with place-relationships relevant to theological verities: ". . . and as concerning the natural body and blood of our Saviour Christ, they are in heaven and not here. It is against the truth of Christ's true natural body, to be in more places than in one, at one time."

A similar problem for today is inherent in the doctrine of Transubstantiation declared by the Fourth Lateran Council in 1215 and further developed by St. Thomas Aquinas. It affirms that at the Eucharist, the "substance" of the bread and the wine changes to the substance of the Body and the Blood of Christ, while the "accidents" (the form) of bread and wine remain. But the categories of Aristotelian physics—which regarded material objects as consisting of a substance and accidents—are not at all true of matter as it is understood in modern physics. Hence the doctrinal definition uses concepts which poorly communicate truth to contemporary minds. And the same is true of the official Lutheran doctrine of Consubstantiation: the co-existence, under the same accidents, of the substance of the bread and wine and the substance of the Body and Blood of Christ. This does *not* mean that the understanding of the nature of matter in the present-day physics is final (often the idolatry of the "liberal" churchmen is the glorification of modern thought, whether in the physical sciences, or in the psychological and social sciences). The point is that the categories of St. Thomas and other scholastic philosophers which make up the *philosophia perennis* are no more perennial (though no less perennial) than those of the going philosophies of other periods of history.

The same point applies to the formulation of the doctrine of the Trinity, regarded as so central to the Christian Faith that the explanation of it requires two-thirds of the lines of the Athanasian Creed, which is introduced by the phrase: "The Catholic Faith is this: That we worship one God in Trinity, and Trinity in Unity." As we shall see in Chapter X, this effort to analyze God was couched in terms of the philosophical currency of the fourth and fifth centuries, involving such concepts as *ousia, hypostasis, substantia,* and *persona.* In the light not only of the change in the meaning of these words but also of the now very much dated character of the philosophical structure which lies behind the words, there is some justification in a humorous response to the phrase in this Creed, "the Father incomprehensible, the Son incomprehensible; and the Holy Ghost incomprehensible": "*The whole thing's incomprehensible!*" This generalization is also true of such phrases as "neither confounding the persons: nor dividing the substance: but by unity of person," from the Athanasian

Creed, and, from the Westminster Confession, "The Father is of none, neither begotten nor proceeding; the Son is eternally begotten of the Father; the Holy Ghost, eternally proceeding from the Father and the Son."[9]

When explanations of the Trinity are made in classical terms and the hearers affirm that they don't understand it, the pat answer is, "Well, it's a mystery." To be sure, any human formulation would be inadequate to encompass the nature of God. But the last time I was preaching to a Chinese congregation, if the sermon had not been followed by a translation, the non-English-speaking members would scarcely have been satisfied to learn that the Bishop was dealing with "a mystery," whether the subject-matter had been the Trinity, the Atonement, or Eternal Life.

Some theologians, aware of the contingent character of the Greek way of thinking which came into the Church with the conversion of the Gentiles, have sought to return to the "verb ideas" customary in biblical and Hebrew thought. They would emphasize the "mighty acts of God" rather than the Greek-oriented concepts used in the reflection on these mighty acts. In line with the predominantly verb character of the Apostles' Creed—and for that matter, a goodly portion of the Nicene Creed—the assumption is that by stressing these verbs the conditional character of philosophies is avoided. Actually, this is not the case. The most significant of these verbs themselves, and the concepts behind them, *presuppose a particular world-view.* "Came down from heaven," "descended," "ascended" are all too comprehensible—and incredible—in this Space Age. So these verbs, too, are dated, and no finality can be attributed to them.

Just as we have seen in the case of biblical fundamentalists, creedal fundamentalists are not as consistently literal as they claim to be. In answer to one who would accept "conceived by the Holy Ghost, born of the Virgin Mary" in a symbolic sense, the fundamentalist would insist that every phrase of the Creed must be believed literally; yet, when pressed, would hardly affirm that

[9] II, § 3.

at the Incarnation Christ literally came down, or that at the Ascension He literally went up.

The Bible, the Creeds, the Confessions of Faith—earthen vessels all; and it is of true religion[10] to declare them so, "that the excellency of the power may be of God, and not of us" (II Cor. 4:7, KJV).

[10] From the Collect for the Seventh Sunday after Trinity, Book of Common Prayer.

III: CODE

M ORE THAN one clergyman has heard a faithful churchwoman say: "My husband never goes to church, but he's the most religious man I've ever known." And, when asked what she means by "religious," she answers, "He is the epitome of the Golden Rule." The validity of this generous estimate of her spouse in both his home and his public life is not the point. What is revealed is a common attitude: the important thing about religion is a code of conduct. For example, the Episcopalian Thomas Jefferson prepared his own version of the Gospels in which the teachings *of* Jesus were included, but teachings *about* Jesus were rigidly excluded.[1]

Most clergy, and certainly all theologians, would deny the view that religion is primarily a code of ethics; yet a survey of preaching content made some years ago by Washington Cathedral's College of Preachers revealed that about 85 per cent of the sermons were on Code, as contrasted to those on Creed and Cult. And in any case, different Churches do set forth various and differing moral rules as absolutes. To the Ten Commandments (which are mutual to all groups), the Roman Catholic Church would add the six Precepts of the Church. Certain denominations

[1] *The Jefferson Bible*, ed. Roche (New York: Clarkson Potter, 1964).

would add strictures against alcoholic beverages, smoking,[2] dancing, and/or the theater; some, in addition to biblical commandments, would add other absolutes, adduced from "natural law"; and nearly all groups, especially in connection with positions taken on social ethics, tend to support their inferences by biblical texts—and some from natural law. The claims of the two great commandments (love of God and neighbor) are generally accepted, but their specific applications are often stated with equal absoluteness.

Often we hear, in sermons and other religious communications, rhetorical references to the "unchanging moral law"; Christian ethics is often portrayed as the abiding standard in a world of change, and perhaps there is added a reference to "crumbling moral values." But how permanent is the Code? Or, to put the question in a way that more nearly touches the concern and thesis of this book: Is its ethics the unchangeable and absolute essence of Christianity?

Of major concern these days is the matter of race relations. So conspicuous now is the official opposition of the Churches to discrimination that it is easy to forget that for the largest segment of its history the Church took slavery for granted and indeed had an ethic about it, namely, (a) masters should be kind and decent toward their slaves; and (b) slaves should be obedient to their masters, whether or not (a) was being fulfilled. The New Testament clearly supports this position (Philemon; I Cor. 7:20-31; I Pet. 2:18). It is true that from time to time, individual Christians, as an altruistic act, freed their slaves or found purchase-money for the freeing of other people's slaves. But there was no over-all challenge to the system. Finally in the eighteenth century the Evangelicals among the Anglicans in England, and later the Abolitionists (largely Congregationalists) in New England, advanced the thesis that the *system* was unethical and campaigned for the abolition of the institution of slavery. Yet for a long time

---

[2] It would appear that they have turned out to be right, at least as far as cigarettes go!

there was little or nothing in the teaching of the Church that challenged discrimination, and the working ethics of the Churches presupposed segregation: Negro churches, Negro schools and colleges, exclusion of Negroes from the beds of Church hospitals, and even the provision of separate Negro jurisdictions in the government of the Church (still obtaining in, e.g., the Methodist Church—where, happily, it is now on the way out). Then with the rise of the "social gospel" (naughty words to the "orthodox"), the conventional view began to be challenged.

Today it is perfectly clear in all quarters that the institution of slavery is sinful; more than that, almost all of the principal Churches, as well as such bodies as the National Council of Churches, are on record as stating that *any* form of discrimination is wrong. It is true, of course, that the Churches remain about the most highly segregated institutions in American life (though country clubs and college fraternities do surpass us); that part of the impetus—particularly on the part of lay people—for the laudable development of Church schools has been the desire to maintain segregation in the face of a more ethical trend on the part of the secular society; and that Negro ministers are rarely considered on their merits in the call of pastors of predominantly white churches, and so forth. Yet the Church's *teaching* is clear—and it is a different teaching from that of previous generations in Christian history. In this very important realm of ethics, how perennial has been the Code?

The Ten Commandments are generally thought to be as "solid as a rock." How solid have they been?

The Second Commandment: Thou shalt not make to thyself any graven image . . . " The beauties—and horrors—of Christian art and iconography witness to a lack of real conviction as to this Commandment.

The Third Commandment: "Thou shalt not take the name of the Lord thy God in vain." The Orthodox Jews are right about the meaning of this injunction: it means that God's "true" name is not to be written or spoken—thus expressing a deeply religious point: He is beyond all labeling. To Christians today it means a quite different (though good) thing: Don't swear.

The Fourth Commandment: "Remember that thou keep holy the Sabbath Day." Since the earliest days of the Jewish-Christian community, most Christian Churches have done nothing in particular about the Sabbath day unless a Holy Day happened to to fall on a Saturday. The big event has been the celebration of the Holy Mysteries on the weekly feast of the Resurrection of Christ, namely, Sunday. The celebration of this day was *not* regarded as a substitute for the fulfillment of the Sabbath requirement in the Commandments (as is indicated by the fact that the first Jewish Christians also observed the Sabbath). The almost universal rule in Christendom is that stated in the Anglican Catechism: "To worship God in His Church every Lord's Day." The day as a whole has not been required to be dedicated to religious exercises or meditation: it is the day for the bullfights in Spanish- and Portuguese-speaking countries; in the United States today, Protestants (except for those who think that Sunday is the same as the Jewish Sabbath) as well as Catholics treat it as a free day (except for Church services) and almost any variety or form of recreation is fine, as is indeed true of Saturday (the Sabbath). In the Anglican Church, this Commandment is read out solemnly once a month (when the rubric requiring it is observed), and the people respond, "Lord, have mercy upon us, and incline our hearts to keep this law," when, in fact, there is no intention whatsoever to keep this law (most of our churches having not so much as a service on that day).

The Fifth Commandment: "Thou shalt not steal." We rather encouraged stealing among the French underground in the last war and the stealing of documents as part of American espionage in the U.S.S.R. is never condemned—nor should it be—by churchmen.

The Sixth Commandment: "Thou shalt not kill (or, "Thou shalt not do murder"). Except for the pacifists, Christian spokesmen in fact have generally endorsed killings in wars of righteousness, in defense of the nation, or "to make the world safe for democracy," and so forth. A new look is being taken at this by Church leaders in light of the potentially catastrophic difference involved in nuclear warfare; but no large Church body has yet affirmed the absoluteness of the Commandment with reference to warfare. Further, the killing of human beings by an individual, in self-defense, is almost universally regarded as right. And capital punishment has been a characteristic feature of "Christian" countries. It has only recently been condemned by some segments of some Churches; and some of us who are against it are not opposed on the basis of an absolute commandment, but on the pragmatic basis that statistics do not seem to indicate that it in fact deters capital crime. Sound or unsound as these various positions may be, there is no use in saying that these killings under special circumstances are not murder because the law of the land does not define them as murder. Such a view is to absolutize societal decisions whereas the only value of an absolute code (if there be such) is to provide a judgment upon societal and individual decisions.

A striking example of the changeability of the Code is found in the teaching of the Anglican Communion on birth control, as expressed through pronouncements issuing from the Lambeth Conference. In 1920, the archbishops and bishops of all the Provinces of the Church throughout the world declared the use of contraceptives sinful; and they declared in 1958, with equal solemnity, that family planning is an obligation, calling for conscientious decisions on the part of each individual couple and endorsing medically approved methods to this end. The Fathers in Lambeth were wiser in 1958 than in 1920; but, in this significant realm of ethics, where is the unchanging Code? (In passing, to those who would think less of our Church for such a reversal in a few decades, we would reply that this illustrates the advantage of a Church's not being infallible.)

Many—and this is not limited to Roman Catholics—ground their conviction about the absoluteness of the Code on "natural law." This phrase is used in two quite different senses: (*a*) the nature and operation of the physical universe, as discerned by the natural sciences, and (*b*) the rules of "correct" human behavior required by the nature of man as discerned by reason— either through generalizations arrived at by deductive reasoning or through generalizations arrived at inductively from patterns of actual human conduct. It is clearly (*b*) and not (*a*) we are talking about here; but this distinction is not always observed by natural-law enthusiasts. They borrow some of their sense of absoluteness in morals from the more apparent absoluteness of natural law in the sense of physical science.

Carefully limiting ourselves to the second meaning ([*b*], above) we find three difficulties with supposed natural law:

1. As I have pointed out elsewhere,[3] when natural-law conclusions are stated specifically enough to be relevant to a given situation, we are in the realm of the conditioned and the contingent; when they are stated broadly enough to be perennial rather than ephemeral, they become platitudinous and uselessly abstract. There seems no way to avoid this Scylla and Charybdis. For example, no one would quarrel in any age or time with the natural-law maxim, "To each according to his due." Such a generalization could doubtless survive all cultural, social, legal, and economic changes in society. But it does not tell us anything. Open is the big question, "What is his due?" On the other hand, "natural law" has been used in different periods of history in support of varying economic systems (feudalism, capitalism, welfare state); varying political systems (the "divine right of kings," democracy); two mutually contradictory positions in the area of religious freedom: both the denial of the rights of religious minorities ("error has no rights") and the affirmation of the right of all men to worship and witness according to their own consciences.

---

[3] Book Article, 51 *Northwestern U. Law Rev.*, pp. 807-12 (1957); see also my comments on the Encyclical *Pacem in Terris* in the Roman Catholic publication, *Continuum* (Summer, 1963), pp. 211-14.

2. In so far as a given natural-law principle is claimed to have been arrived at inductively, i.e., by observation as to how mankind generally behaves, sociological, anthropological, psychological, and historical studies have increasingly made evident that various sizable groups of mankind over considerable periods of time have behaved in quite varying ways on every subject to be comprehended within the realm of morals. This is not to say that all of these patterns are equally good; but they have existed and do exist, and this fact defeats the hope of finding in a universal consensus support for given applications of moral law—however sound we may deem them to be.

3. In so far as natural law purports to be derived from deductive reason, we find in every case that the conclusion of the syllogism is already built into the major or the minor premise, which in turn is based directly on faith or derived from a precedent syllogism or syllogisms whose major or minor premises are based on faith. This is true of theological premises *per se*; and it is likewise true of the first premises of a natural-law ethic. The difficulty can be seen underlying the present position of the Roman Catholic Church as to the use of contraceptives. Reduced to syllogistic form:

Major premise: Artificial frustration of the primary purpose of a natural process is sinful.

Minor premise: The primary purpose of sexual intercourse is procreation.

Conclusion: Ergo, the artificial frustration (i.e., by contraception) of procreation in connection with sexual intercourse is sinful.

The major premise is a good example of a natural-law principle, and is broad enough to escape the charge of contingency; consequently, it is so platitudinous that it tells us nothing. Its possible meaning is entirely dependent upon the meaning of the key words "natural process" and "frustration."

The minor premise *does* tell us something. Whence its support? Inductive inquiry? Does observation—anthropological and psychological—of various cultures in various periods entirely support the claim that the desire for procreation has been always and everywhere the only primary basis for the sex drive? And if the *is*, is to be equated with the *ought* (hardly a premise congenial with Roman Catholic ethical thought in general), the fact is that there has been a long history of conscious efforts—with varying degrees of success—designed to thwart the fulfillment of this primary purpose through the widespread use of birth control measures—involving incidentally, a high percentage of the Roman Catholic population in the United States and in a number of other countries.

So the minor premise ("The primary purpose of sexual intercourse is procreation") cannot be proved inductively. Can it be proved deductively, i.e., by reasoning from previously proved premises? Where would one possibly find such premises, ones *not* based on faith? Thus, the minor premise of the above syllogism is based on faith. Pointing out the fact that it is so based is not meant in itself to be a criticism, since the alternative premise accepted in my own Church on the subject is also based on faith. We affirm that there are at least two primary purposes for sexual intercourse: procreation and the sacramental expression of, and means toward, the unity of the couple. This differs from the Roman Catholic proposition, in that while in the latter Church there is increasing recognition that the second factor is a true purpose, at the present reading it is for them at most a secondary purpose: procreation remains *the* primary purpose.

Empirical observation as to what sexuality has actually meant in human life might make our principle seem more plausible than the Roman Catholic principle; nevertheless, both are equally accepted by faith. In this realm, as well as in the realm of theological premises, since a leap of faith is involved, we can only say that it is wiser to take the leap toward that which is more plausible, not toward that which is more implausible. But my point in using this illustration is not to *prove* the minor premise which underlies the Anglican position on contraception, or even to establish that it is preferable to the Roman Catholic minor premise; rather, the analysis is meant to show that neither conclusion (theirs or ours) can claim the support of an unchanging "natural law" whether sought to be proved by empirical observation or reason, or purportedly derived inductively or deductively.

In other words, "natural law" is simply a holy noise or a color-words phrase used forensically in support of a current position held on other bases. It is fruitless to look here for an absolute grounding for ethical positions.

One of the other topics which came up at the Lambeth Conference of 1958 is also instructive. It was proposed that a resolution endorsing monogamy be adopted. Many of us attending the sessions were astonished because of the apparent obviousness of the absolute involved. But we learned something about marital situations in the lands of some of the new African nations, in a social structure where polygamy is the order of the day and where there is no independent career role for women. Suppose such a wife is converted to Christianity. Can she be baptized and confirmed and continue in her marital status? Or to be joined to the Body of Christ must she leave the harem? Departure may well mean starvation—or prostitution, if she is to survive. A Christian outcome? Or suppose that the husband is converted. Is he, as a condition of baptism, to "draw straws," dismiss the overplus, and reduce them to penury? Or perhaps a *tertium quid*: could he let them keep their place in the household and be single-minded in his sexual expression? Apart from the existential unlikelihood of maintaining such a designed discipline, what about the passage in the Lord's Prayer, "lead us not into temptation"? Further, would not this solution deny something to the rejected wives? May they not have what in Anglo-Saxon law we call "the right of consort" to which the husband committed himself, as part of their fulfillment? A Christian outcome? The solution in some African dioceses is to permit the polygamous husband-believer to be baptized on his deathbed; but converted wives may remain *in statu quo* and be baptized now.

Somewhat closer to home is the question of remarriage after divorce. In regard to this increasingly recurrent problem, not only do various Churches differ; particular Churches have changed their rules over the centuries, and within a particular Church interpretations can differ in different areas. Jesus stated the ideal, on which all certainly agree: a marriage should be lifelong. But when in fact a marriage has definitely failed, then what? To this question there is no consistent single answer.

All along, two quite different basic attitudes have been operative in the Church in one form or another. To employ a distinction made in the Preface, one is existential and the other is ontological. The existential approach assumes that just as a spouse can die, leaving the other party free to remarry,[4] a marriage can die—with the same result. The ontological approach assumes that the marriage bond is an indestructible fact, whatever has happened between the parties—including separation or divorce through civil courts.

The first example of the "spiritual-death" approach is reflected in the "adultery exception" in St. Matthew's account of Jesus' statement against divorce (19:9). Most New Testament scholars now regard these words as a later interpolation; apparently they represent an early bit of canon law on the subject, which was followed thereafter, at least in the Eastern Church, by the recognition of other bases—e.g., cruelty and desertion—for declaring a marriage spiritually dead.

Another early use of what in effect is the spiritual-death approach—still alive in the Roman Catholic Church—is the "Pauline privilege," based on an unelaborated sentence from the writings of the Apostle: "If the unbelieving partner desires to separate, let it be so: in such a case [the believing partner] is not bound" (I Cor. 7:15, RSV). This has been interpreted to mean that a postmarital conversion can supply the convert a ground for an ecclesiastical declaration that the previous tie is no longer binding —a view apparently in conflict with the simultaneously recognized

---

[4] For a while in the early Church this was not entirely the case: permanent widowhood was endorsed.

principle that marriage is a *natural* sacrament, of which the partners are the ministers, regardless of religious connection.

But the Roman Catholic Church has usually affirmed the onto-logical approach: The marriage bond is indestructible. Hence the right to remarry must be based on a finding that the first union was not a marriage at all. Thus there began to be recognized various impediments to matrimony, ranging from such obvious grounds as bigamy and fraud to such fancifully pseudo-incestuous ones as having been one's wife's godfather.

In the Anglican Communion the annulment theory is uni-versally recognized, but with different lists of impediments in different places (the American Episcopal Church, for example, has added "psychological defects") and with a willingness in some Provinces to make an ecclesiastical adjudication of nullity and reluctance to do so in others (in which case a civil decree of an-nulment is the only basis for remarriage). But there is division in the ranks as to the availability of the spiritual-death approach—even in the Episcopal Church, where the wording of the current canon law clearly leaves room for it (App. A). Whether or not a given divorcé could successfully jump these hurdles (varying, as they do, in height in different dioceses), if he goes ahead and gets married but still clings to the Church generally he will in due time be restored to communicant status—often also with a service "blessing" the new marriage (which is all, religiously speaking, that the marriage service itself is anyway). By this action the Church implies that the party is not living in sin—even though the first marriage bond had been viewed as indissoluble! More consistent logically, though less helpful pastorally, is the contrary position of the Roman Catholic Church: no restoration to Communion with-out abandoning sexual relations with the new spouse.

Different again—and much less complex—is the attitude of most Protestant Churches today: divorced persons may simply be remarried at the discretion of the minister.[5]

Even more fundamental is the pattern of change in the

[5] In the United Presbyterian Church a one-year waiting period is required, unless dispensed by the Presbytery.

Churches' attitude toward sex in general, already suggested, to some extent, in connection with sex in marriage. In this development can be discerned three phases.

1. From the early Church on, with some support in the New Testament (e.g., I Cor. 7) and with ample support in the Fathers,[6] procreation was *the* purpose of sex,[7] marriage was inferior to celibacy, and the act of conception always involved sin.[8] It would appear that about the first positive word, in any theological writing in English, endorsing sex in broader terms was spoken by Jeremy Taylor, a married priest of the Church of England, in the seventeenth century.[9] The previous attitude toward intercourse is still recited in the marriage service of the Church of England: "It was ordained for a remedy against sin, and to avoid fornication, that such persons as have not the gift of continence might marry and keep themselves undefiled. . . ."[10]

2. A nobler basis for intercouse is more and more characteristic of the Church in the present era. The procreative function is not ignored, though the appropriateness of its suspension is recognized and the "lesser of two evils" approach is rarely voiced. Now recognized as a primary purpose of intercourse is its sacramental function. A sacrament is "an outward and visible sign of an inward and spiritual grace." In a sacrament each of the elements (the outward and the inward) is both cause and effect. In, for example, Holy Communion, the partaking of bread and wine is the *expression* of the congregation's union in Christ; it is also a *means of grace*, that is, a way in which this union is effected. So in marriage. The physical act expresses the spiritual unity of the couple; at the same time it is a means of nurturing and strengthen-

---

[6] E.g., St. Augustine was troubled that intercourse involved "bestial movements."

[7] St. Jerome granted a limited value to the sexual act: from it could be produced more virgins.

[8] See more fully D. S. Bailey, *Sexual Relation in Christian Thought* (New York: Harper & Row, 1959).

[9] *The Rule and Exercises of Holy Living.*

[10] Book of Common Prayer (Church of England), the Exhortation in the Solemnization of Matrimony.

ing that unity.[11] Concurrent with this line of thought has been increasing recognition that marital intercourse is good and that the marriage state need not yield first place to celibacy.

3. During the revolution in thinking about sex in marriage, it was simply assumed by all parties that any sexual expression outside of marriage was taboo. Is it? Actually, unadvertised, this question had long been asked—and answered in different ways—in private conversations among the clergy and in pastoral conferences with individual laity. In the last few years it has also been cropping up in public—not just in pornographic literature, but in serious theological and ethical essays and sermons.[12] No new code has been proclaimed, but clearly detectable is a shift from an ontological basis ("absolutely not," "under no circumstances") to an existential basis ("it depends"). As of this writing the existential view is being expressed cautiously (for reasons one can well understand). Still the literature of the current openness touches masturbation, premarital relations, extramarital relations and free-consenting adult homosexual expression. The general tenor of the authors is still reticent; but the underlying basis has shifted: the individual factors—and the projection of the possible outcome—in each situation are what count. The vector-analysis would caution restraint; but not necessarily always.

In summarizing these three views (the first obtained for the largest part of the Church's history) I am not here arguing for any one of them. The point is that we do *not* see in the Church's

[11] See more fully the Report of the 1958 Lambeth Conference, 2.141-ff.; the volume on ethics in the Episcopal Church's teaching series—S. Bayne, *Christian Living* (New York: Seabury Press, 1957), Chap. 7; my *Beyond Anxiety* (New York: Charles Scribner's Sons, 1953), Chap. 5, and *Doing the Truth* (Garden City, N.Y.: Doubleday and Co., 1955), Chap. 13.

[12] See, e.g., H. A. Williams, Dean of Trinity College, Cambridge, in *Soundings*, ed. A. Vidler (Cambridge: Cambridge University Press, 1962), pp. 81-82; *Towards a Christian View of Sex*, ed. Haron (Friends Home Service Comm., 1963); J. A. T. Robinson, *Honest to God* (London: S.C.M.; Philadelphia: Westminster, 1963); Robinson, *Christian Morals Today* (London: S.C.M., 1964); Canon Douglas Rhymes (of Southwark Cathedral), *No New Morality* (London: Constable, 1964). *Cf.* Lunn and Lean, *The New Morality* (London: Blandford, 1964) which summarizes and attacks the new trend.

attitude toward sex and marriage an example of "unchanging moral law."

One last example can be briefly stated. For a long period of the Church's history, charging any interest on loans was sinful: it was the sin of usury. Today "usury" has come to mean charging an *illegal* rate of interest. And what contemporary Church labels as necessarily sinful the work of its communicants in the banking profession? Even the Church itself takes interest on loans. (This is true of the revolving loan fund of our own diocese, on which interest is charged to congregations—and nonpayment is the only sin we perceive in such transactions.)

The image which is generally maintained by the Church is that there is an absolute Code (whether it derives from the Bible, natural law, reason, or from sheer ecclesiastical authority) and that this Code is to be the judge of changing tendencies and practices in various societies and cultures. Actually, a more candid review of the history of the relationship between the Church's ethics and societal matters, including the civil law, would suggest that the relationship between judged and judging is just as often the reverse.[13]

[13] As to the formative effect of law on morals, see my *Beyond the Law* (Garden City, N.Y.; Doubleday and Co., 1963), Chap. 4, and, more fully, E. Cahn, *The Moral Decision* (Bloomington, Ind.: Indiana University Press, 1955).

IV: CULT

T HE MATTERS which can be grouped under the heading of Cult would seem to offer less opportunity for absolutism than those which come under Creed or Code. It is true that here such rigidity as has obtained is easier to discern and to modify; but, on the other hand—and this is often overlooked by theologians—it is in the general area of worship that most people have their most obvious relationship with the Church. For many, their religion *is* the Sunday service and rites that touch the family life; Creed and Code are simply part of what is talked about in the services—with little bearing on attitudes and decision-making throughout the week. Since for most churchgoers, especially for the theologically unreflective, Cult *is* the religion, it is not surprising that rigidities and idolatries have developed in this area as well. For example:

1. A certain rector introduced the custom of having an acolyte carry the American flag in the procession which opened the service—the flag then being solemnly placed in the sanctuary. After his retirement, the custom was discontinued under the new rector. The reasons—sound or unsound—are not important here. The new rector may have felt that the ceremony was inconsistent with the fact that what was to follow was a service of the Holy Catholic Church, not that of an American sect; he may have felt that the small sanctuary was too crowded; he may have been short of

acolytes; he may simply have forgotten about the matter. But this change brought about a great contention in the parish. At a home meeting a group vowed that they would not return to worship in that church until the flag was restored, and drafted an appeal to the bishop. They did not articulate any theological or liturgical grounding for their position (e.g., it could have been suggested that carrying the flag and placing it in the sanctuary presented the offering of the life of the nation to God, like the offering of the alms and the oblations). Rather, in addition to thinking the rector unpatriotic—and perhaps under some Communist influence—they underlined the assertions that "the flag has *always* been used in the service" (the newcomers knew no better, and the oldtimers had short memories), and that "it is done everywhere else" (a survey of six surrounding Episcopal churches would have shown that two used the flag, one used it only on patriotic or special occasions, and three never used it). To these people *this* was an absolute.

2. The new pastor, in his eagerness to "make the Faith plain" in preaching, lapsed into heresy after heresy: on the Trinity, Sabellianism ("God has shown himself to us in three ways . . ."); on Salvation, Pelagianism ("If you do good all your life you will be everlastingly rewarded . . ."); and on Christ, everything from Adoptionism ("Jesus was so good that God chose Him to . . .") to Apollinarianism (an overly simplified Jesus = God). None of this caused so much as a ripple. But when he adopted a more formal service and the interior of the church began to reflect a more traditional appearance, the fat was in the fire. Often heard were the phrases "We've *never* . . ." and "We've *always* . . . ."

In such contentions the historical sense is lost, and the recent past is elevated into the category of the unchanging. Take hymnody: many of the familiar hymns are quite subjective and sentimental in their religious psychology—"Just as I am . . . ," "Good night, sweet Jesus," "Rock of ages, cleft for me . . . let me hide. . . ." By contrast, the lyrics of the hymns of the medieval and Reformation periods generally are more objective, more focused on God and His mighty acts, and their accompanying music is less sentimental. Yet attempts to restore the older type of hymn are frequently met with "We want to stick to the *old* hymns"— a position tenable only if there has been no glance at the dates of composition which most hymnals provide. The protester has finalized what is old to *him*—the very subjectivity that the introduction of really old hymns is meant to counterbalance.

Or take the attitudes on prayer: the plaintiffs and defendants in contests about kneeling *vs.* sitting for prayer overlook the fact that both positions are relatively recent. *Standing* for prayer is "the old way."

In the Episcopal Church the standard for correctness can be variously the Roman rite before recent reforms, the Sarum rite which was widespread in late medieval England, the actual or imagined usages of the early Church, the latest experiment of the Liturgical Movement, the way things were done in the seminary chapel, or the way they have always been done at St. Swithin's-in-the-Swamp (see App. B). The very existence of so many conflicting norms, with roots in different periods of history and with different aesthetic contexts, should suggest that no one of them has any finality.

Hardly less fictitious is the absoluteness which is attributed to particular views as to the number, nature, form, and indispensability of various sacraments and rites. For example, a good case can be made for adult "believer's baptism" (being a Christian is a commitment—though in practice in Baptist churches what is involved is *deferred* infant baptism); and a good case can be made for infant baptism (grace is operative in the whole family of God). But neither point excludes the other; hence it is not compromise, but a recognition of the incompleteness of all human expressions of meaning, that supports the Church of South India's allowing either practice, in the discretion of each local church.

Most Churches regard the Holy Communion as more than a symbolic commemoration: the Divine reality is really present (some call this the doctrine of the Real Presence). But as to the mechanics of relating chosen physical objects to the Presence, a number of different views are held by different traditions today and have existed in the same Church in different periods of history. Each of these views is a refraction of the truth, but the contenders have always tended to insist that their particular theory or practice is the *only* true view. The same mentality displays itself even as to the elements to be used. In support of leavened bread is claimed the necessity of the breaking of one loaf; in support of wafers is the assumption that the Last Supper took place on the Feast of the Unleavened Bread.[1] In support of grape juice is the fact that Jesus used the common things in the diet of His day, and in today's culture (or, more accurately, the pietistic subculture within the American culture), fruit juice, not wine, so qualifies; in support of wine is the fact that Jesus used it (it is interesting that the Episcopal Church, which declares wine essential, is fundamentalist about little else in the Bible).

The same rigidity in the face of change and variety is seen in connection with confirmation, private confession, the anointing of the sick, and polity, particularly with reference to the structure and genealogy of the ministry. Absolutism here has divided Christians and threatens to continue to divide them (see App. B).

An interesting example of an illusory absolute in the realm of polity is found in one of the grounds for the declaration of the invalidity of Anglican Orders by Pope Leo XIII in the Bull *Apostolicae Curae* in 1896, namely, the lack of provision for the *traditio instrumentorum* in the Anglican rite of ordination to the priesthood. In fact this is a meaningful ceremony (in my diocese, for example, we deliver to the ordinand a chalice and paten along with the Bible at the words, "Take thou Authority to preach the Word of God, and to minister the holy Sacraments in the Congregation . . ."). The Roman Catholics themselves, however, have discovered that the *traditio instrumentorum* was a rather late

[1] The Gospels are in conflict on this; but if the assumption about unleavened bread is correct—and important—then why not matzos?

medieval ceremony. If it is essential, even the Pope's orders are invalid!

As to the genealogical aspect of polity, the ministry of virtually all Churches have some kind of succession. Ordination is by laying on of hands performed by the ministers who have been similarly ordained by others. This practice is suitably symbolic of the on-going, organic character of the visible Church. But some insist that orders not conferred by bishops in the historic succession are invalid. Some say that such orders, while real and effective in some sense, are yet invalid; others say that episcopal ordination, while nonessential, is an important element in a united Church; others say it is not this important, but is a good thing; others deny even that.

Just as in the case of the declaration of Papal Infallibility at the Vatican Council of 1870, there is a basic theological difficulty in attributing ultimacy to any such human structure as ordination ceremonies. If there is nothing "beyond" the *ex cathedra* pro-nouncement of a particular bishop by which it can be judged or reformed, then in that particular role the bishop is deified—divinity *meaning* the ultimate, that beyond which you cannot go. Likewise with the designation of the historic episcopate as the only sure and reliable channel of God's grace; likewise with the ultimacy of the threefold ministry of bishops, priests, and deacons. There are also biblical and historical difficulties; e.g., (*a*) literal, tactual succession from the apostles down to modern bishops is in fact impossible to prove—whatever inference one might wish to draw in regard to what went on in the first century of the Church's life; (*b*) the emergence of the presbyterate as a separate order is not apparent in biblical times; and (*c*) both congregational and presbyteral commissioning of bishops seems to have been extant in the very early Church. The Preface to the Anglican Ordinal says, "It is evident to all men, diligently reading Holy Scripture and ancient Authors, that from the Apostles' time there have been these Orders of Ministers in Christ's Church—Bishops, Priests, and Deacons." But as Dr. Walter Lowrie has pointed out, "With good reason the Preface to our Ordinal emphasizes the need of 'diligence' in reading Holy Scripture and ancient authors with a view to detecting the 'evident' truth that from the Apostles' time there have been three orders of ministers in the Church."[2]

Further, the fluctuation of the functions and the respective roles of bishops, presbyters, and deacons over the centuries makes it difficult to attribute an absolute—as contrasted to a functional—character to the respective offices in the Church.

The tendency toward exclusivism in this latter regard is a most conspicuous barrier to the efforts now under way to achieve Church unity. The plain fact is that no minister of Christ,[3] as a condition of unity, is going to affirm that until hands were laid upon him by a bishop in the historic succession he was nothing but a layman; in other words, he cannot affirm with integrity—in the light of his actual ministry as a means of grace in the Word and Sacraments—that the episcopate is necessary for ordination as a minister of Christ. Nor is there any reason that Anglican negotiators for unity should require such an affirmation, since within the fold of our Church it is licit to hold any one of three views of the episcopate (App. B, ¶ 7), two of which do not denigrate others' ministries; and hence it would be unreasonable to erect higher fences for those outside of our Communion than we do for those within.[4]

[2] *Dr. Lowrie of Princeton and Rome*, ed. H. Johnson (New York: Seabury Press, 1957), p. 71.

[3] Ministers of other denominations are recognized as "ministers of Christ" by Canon 36 of the Episcopal Church.

[4] The soundest current plans for Church unity are the Ceylon Scheme, the North India-Pakistan Plan, the Australian Plan, and the proposal outlined by Dr. Eugene Carson Blake, the Stated Clerk of the United Presbyterian Church, in a sermon at the Cathedral Church in San Francisco, which has resulted in official conversations among six Churches. In each of these it is proposed to recognize the reality of all ministers; to unify the ministries by mutual laying on of hands, recognizing the existential reality and incompleteness of all of our ministries in a divided Church, and relying on the Holy Spirit to provide whatever grace, character, order, or authority may be required for exercise of fuller ministry in the United Church. (In the Church of South India, now fifteen years old, episcopal ordination was provided for the future, but nonepiscopally ordained ministers have continued their duties side by side with episcopally ordained clergy.)

But views of the ministry are not the only barriers to Church unity. A corollary to the thesis of this book is that there is no essential difference in the teaching of the principal Christian Churches. But it would be naïve to assert that there are no differences which this Church or that—or some members thereof—regard as essential.

Yet where there are differences, the fact is that various portions of the Church have done pragmatically what they have thought best at various times in history. We must remember that God can break through with His grace, whatever the shapes and sizes of channels we have provided. The important thing is that we not absolutize what are pragmatically designed channels. For example, though confirming is a large part of my work as a bishop, it is an open secret that we do not know exactly what Confirmation is. Nevertheless, I do not hesitate to perform it, since I do trust that God is in it—effective for us owing to our intentions—trust that it is a means of grace. If that is the case, I do not need to know precisely, in the light of various historical fluctuations concerning the relationship of Confirmation to Baptism and to the Eucharist, what the accurate answer is about this particular sacramental machinery as found at this particular period of history and in my particular Communion. And so with the other rites and ceremonies of the Church. God is present in it all and is ever ready to be in relationship with those who seek to be open to Him.

No Church, even for the sake of unity, should sacrifice what it deems to be an essential of the Faith. On the other hand, we have no right to boggle at unity because of any nonessential differences, or (in the light of the early Christian community's understanding of our Lord's will for His Church) to block the fulfillment of the hope "that they may all be one . . . , that the world may believe that thou hast sent me . . . and hast loved them" (John 17:21-23, RSV).

V: WHAT
CHRISTIANITY IS

WHAT *is* essential, absolute, unchanging about Christianity? What is the heart of the matter? In short, what is a Christian?

We will hope to come to an answer by analyzing what can be the most crucial experience in an individual human life. Should the essential thing about Christianity correspond with the essential of that experience, then our conviction about Christianity will have been grounded in self-authenticating reality and there will have been provided at one and the same time a sound theology and a persuasive apologetic for that theology—in terms of the test of *plausibility* set forth in the first chapter.

William James in *The Varieties of Religious Experience*[1] distinguishes between two types of personalities: the once-born and the twice-born. The former may be a person born into a Christian family who, as he matures, gradually enters more and more into its convictions and ideals; he may have some ups and downs as to belief and conduct, but in general there is a stability in his life and a continuity in his relationship to God and in his earthly perspective. Now this is a good thing; in fact, the Church has arranged its work with the purpose and hope that this very thing will happen; at least it is presupposed in the programs of Christian

---

[1] New Hyde Park, N.Y.: University Books, 1963.

nurture offered through the more classical types of Christianity. Just as in the case of modern social security, what is intended is cradle-to-grave coverage—and beyond the grave in the continuity of eternal life.

But a second type of personality development has repeatedly manifested itself: the twice-born experience of a definitive down-and-up episode. If at some point in his personal history it has been said about a man that he has "hit bottom," it can mean a number of things:

Perhaps ennui has come to an intense and unbearable point. All those aspects of his life which have been thrilling and exciting —or at least enjoyable—in his work, his pleasures, his friends, more and more bore him. Having throughout life—as all persons do— regarded or minimized this or that with a "So what?" he now is asking the big "So what?" Nothing matters. The ephemeral and repetitive character of everything has "got him down."

Or, having been spared open cynicism and emptiness by an abiding—if not sturdy—religious belief, he now "loses his faith." This may come about through a great disappointment—in a person or persons or in a turn of events; or it may have come about he knows not how: he just finds himself not believing; he is overcome with a sense of meaninglessness; in the center of his existence there is a great vacuum.

Or, he has gradually become involved in a pattern of living which has brought him to the pit: for example, an addiction like alcohol. He has not recognized the danger as such; he has been well equipped with the usual excuses, uttered the usual re-assurances to those closest to him and concerned about the matter. But finally an emotional crisis occurs where he literally hits bottom. The circumstances may have been such that a public or semi-public scandal results in his losing everything. Or, by chance or Providence, there may have been more protective—and protect-able—circumstances. But it is all the same as far as what has happened to him inside is concerned. Brushed away all at once are his excuses, the basis for his reassurances to others, his sense of security and surrounding supports—and, most of all, his sense of confidence in himself.

Whichever of these three—or other—ways the climax has come about, it is in a definite moment of time; it is datable. We will call this *Moment I.*

Then, in many cases (not all, by any means) there comes *Moment II.* Something rises as from the inside—and he rises with it. It could be something dramatic by way of a form of revelation; more likely it will be a simple quiet conviction that everything is going to be all right. In the case of ennui it could be a conviction as to the intrinsic beauty and worthwhileness of things; in the case of meaninglessness in could be a solid sense of faith; in the case of the problem of alcohol, it can be a straightforward *inner* conviction that "I am not going to drink any more."

The word "inner" is emphasized because this experience differs so markedly from that of persuasion from the outside. A man increasingly depressed under the tastelessness of things may have articulated his ennui to those nearest to him and heard many cheerful words; he may even have given outer assent to these sentiments. If he has lost his faith, he may have heard arguments in favor of the plausibility of religious belief, and his mind even assented to such propositions. In the case of an addiction, he may have been lectured (he doubtless regarded it as "nagging") by his wife and others and has probably from time to time made promises—and sincere ones. Through will power, and little programs of conformity, he has often held the line. With some aplomb he has even managed to function. Still, none of this has really "worked."

But after Moment II, the crucial time of inner change, there is no struggle. From now on, to take the addictive example, he does not *want* to drink. In his conformity it is not a case of his being against himself—a divided man. His own self is settled on this score. And not only this score: whatever the root cause, the response all comes down to the same thing underneath—a quiet serenity of assurance. In the continuing "changes and chances of this mortal life" (they do not necessarily abate) he is thereafter not basically disturbed. He knows *new life*, he is a new being, he is *born again*.

This approach to religious conversion is well known to psychiatrists, whatever their own religious orientation. They recognize that Moment I and Moment II can happen to a person either in terms of religious symbols or without any religious symbolism at all; but whatever their school of thought, they would readily label this dynamic as a *religious experience*. To take the more vivid of the three examples above, the general reaction of people to a friend's stopping drinking is, "Oh well, he'll go back to it." This is a canny observation; in most cases it tells the truth. If the man's decision was "from outside" himself it divides him against himself; it is a case, to use Freudian terms, of the superego so dominating the ego that the id is locked in chains. But the superego and id can themselves be so transformed that they are in accord with the ego's integration of the personality; and as psychiatrists readily recognize (and others have known through experience), such a person will not easily go back to the "old pattern." Even if he slips once or twice, he readily perceives how out of character this pattern now is for him and his increased distaste for these tokens of the old life buttress his resistance.

Saul's fanatic hatred toward those of the Jewish community who believed Jesus to be the Messiah and his painfully legalistic self-righteousness finally were shown to be genuine blindness when on the Damascus road he faced the judgment of Him who was Truth and Love. When his sight was restored at the home of Ananias he was a new man: Saul became Paul. Ever thereafter in his new life, crises increased rather than decreased; but he could utter such words as, "by honour and dishonour, by evil report and good report: as deceivers, and yet true; as unknown, and yet well known; as dying, and, behold, we live; as chastened, and not killed; as sorrowful, yet alway rejoicing; as poor, yet making many rich; as having nothing, and yet possessing all things" (II Cor. 6:8-10, KJV).

When St. Augustine's preoccupation with worldly ambition and sensual pleasure went sour, he felt a sense of great emptiness: As he sat quietly in a garden, he was able to "take in" that which he had doubtless read before; now he could really hear it: ". . . not in chambering and wantonness, not in strife and envying. But put ye on the Lord Jesus Christ . . ." (Rom. 13:13-14, KJV). Thus the new man was born.

Martin Luther, preoccupied with a sense of guilt, going up the *scala sancta* on his knees to earn favor with God, was then ready to receive the full force of the words of the Apostle whose epistles he was studying: "The just shall live by faith." So he rose and went down the stairs knowing that he was accepted then and there, knowing the secret of self-acceptance in the light of God's acceptance of the unacceptable. He was a new man now; and he was apt for the great task of the Reformation.

Many are the variations on the theme. The configuration of each problem is different, the shape of the pit is different, the way in which the element of resurrection occurs—and the form its takes— is different.

How does one who has such an experience *maintain* his aplomb? What is the source of his perseverance in the new life? The answer is: *He remembers.* He remembers Moment I and Moment II; he recalls his death, his resurrection. This recollection may be most vivid and pointed in times of crisis; situations arise which in the old life could have sunk him—would have brought him to despair, back to the bottle or what not; yet the remembering is actually always with him; he never consciously reflects on his new strength without the sense of the presence with him *now* of the reality of these two Moments of the past. They have become part of him and are like breathing. He continually re-enters that which was at a given place and time, but which has a permanent abiding reality, that which is *for once and for all.* Such a man has passed from bondage into freedom; he has died and risen again.

In the light of this crucial and dramatic capacity for human experience the question can be reasked, What is a Christian? But first we should ask, What is a Jew? Marcion in the second century sought to achieve a discontinuity between Judaism and Christianity. He was declared a heretic; but a practical working

Marcionism has tended to infect Christianity ever since. And the result has always been the thinning out of the Christian message and the lessening of its credibility. While one can be a Jew without being a Christian, one cannot be a Christian without being a Jew. Hence, we ask, *What is a Jew?*

Jews have many beliefs, affirmations, moral laws, and liturgical practices. Were there time and space, these could be shown, under the headings of Creed, Code, and Cult, to be relative and historically conditioned, variant, and changing. But what lies behind all this? What is a Jew—essentially? *A Jew is one who remembers, who remembers two things: the bondage in Egypt and the exodus through the Red Sea waters.* This remembering is the theme of the principal feast of Judaism, the Passover, as celebrated movingly at the Seder; these manifestations of God are remembered at every Sabbath service as part of the continuing consciousnss of the devout Jew. Through that which is temporal and historical, the eternal God is revealed in relation to man's condition. The abiding and the eternal is perceived. The very character of the eternal God is seen and trusted.

Now we can ask, What is a Christian? *A Christian is one who remembers, who remembers two things: the death and the Resurrection of Christ.* This is ever commemorated in the first of the Christian festivals to be established—Easter day. And weekly since the beginning, Christians have gathered every Sunday in celebration of these manifestations of God. In them we see revealed the same God Who is the father of Abraham, Isaac, and Jacob and Who is displayed in the Exodus. It is thus no accident that traditional lections and hymns at Eastertide recall the deliverance of the Jews from bondage; for example:

> God hath brought his Israel
> Into joy from sadness;
> Loosed from Pharaoh's bitter yoke
> Jacob's sons and daughters;
> Led them with unmoistened foot
> Through the Red Sea waters.
>> —ST. JOHN OF DAMASCUS (eighth century)

As we shall see, this remembering is the theme that is at the heart of the two great sacraments—Baptism and Holy Communion. Thus two historical facts, in a given time and place relating to a given Individual, are for the Christian abiding—and eternal.

How do these things become the center of genuine belief to men today? Let us return to the distinction between the once-born and the twice-born.

The twice-born will ever remember Moment I and Moment II, datable events in his own life. His new life ever after Moment II is sustained by this remembering. This being as real to him as the very center of his existence, this personal experience can be the entry to belief in the two Moments of cosmic significance. In His Passion and death Jesus Christ really "hit bottom" in the Garden of Gethsemane ("O Father, if it be thy will, let this cup pass from me") and on the Cross ("My God, my God, why hast thou forsaken me?"); this Moment I corresponds to the Moment I—whatever form it took—in the life of the twice-born individual. And on the third day Christ rose gloriously from the dead; this Moment II corresponds to Moment II—whatever form it took—in the life of the twice-born individual. For *him* it is not difficult to believe that that type of experience which is central to his own being—the support of his new life—is grounded in the very nature of things, that it is the deepest way God is related to people, that it is the central way the Ultimate Ground of all being is related to those made in His image.

A truly twice-born man *knows* that death and resurrection is at the heart of his reality, and hence it is not likely to strike him as something quixotic or exceptional that it is at the heart of Ultimate Reality. Rather, it is likely to strike him as the way things should be—or actually, the way they are. Instead of something incredible, it is most plausible. He can match up his own experience, from his own two great events, with this revelation of God in Christ and he becomes even more stable in the change which has been wrought in him, sensing the eternal significance in his passing days. All men are made for this, called to this.

Jesus said, "I have come that men might have life and have it more abundantly"—not just twice-born men, but men.

Here we must distinguish the matter of belief from the matter of actual experience. From apostolic times on, many people who themselves have not dramatically hit bottom and risen again (have not experienced a radical defeat and a datable lifting up of their lives into a new dimension) have come to accept Christianity because they have responded in admiration and hope upon hearing the proclamation of Moment I and Moment II in Jesus Christ. They have found this credible because they have witnessed new life in others who have accepted Jesus Christ. The first testimony came from the Apostles and those who knew these facts directly and who had been changed, but then it began to come from those who had been won by the living power of their witness. One who did not know Jesus, the unknown author of I John, yet can write in terms of direct experience, "It was there from the beginning; we have heard it; we have seen it with our own eyes; we have looked upon it, and felt it with our own hands; and it is of this we tell. Our theme is the word of life. This life was made visible; we have seen it and bear our testimony; we here declare to you the eternal life which dwelt with the Father and was made visible to us. What we have seen and heard we declare to you, so that you and we together may share in a common life, that life which we share with the Father and his son Jesus Christ. And we write this in order that the joy of us all may be complete" (I John 1:1-4, NEB). In this manner, all through the centuries, has come belief—for most who have believed, and believe. But how may such a one come into the new life itself? Must he himself duplicate the experience and be himself twice-born? Must he die in order that he may rise again?

The Christian Faith has an answer to this, and it is part of the heart of the matter. First, let us look at the psychodynamics of the process. In alcoholism, for example, it is generally known that excess alcohol is not *the* problem (much as it contributes to the maintenance of the problem). Underneath, always, is a deeper psychological problem; generally speaking, it is the lack of integration of the personality. Alcohol, in its capacity to numb some things, provides an exaggerated sense of power in other things. Thereby one can achieve a false sense of integration and well-being. The effectiveness of this palliative depends upon keeping a certain level of intoxication; when the level is exceeded then the artificial sense of the proportion of things is destroyed and the "demons" are really let loose from the unconscious. On the other hand, when the intake drops below the level, integration temporarily ceases; the diffusion of the foci of the man's existence is evident again. He is torn, schizoid (loosely speaking), and depressed. But by experience he knows the remedy of both the plus and the minus in regard to intake; thus the cycle goes on and on.

It is only when the configuration of events and the amount of intake concur to bring about disastrous consequences (or serious risk of the same, fortuitously averted) or the fear—well- or ill-grounded—of irreparable damage, along with a deep sense of shame for the incapacity to cope—indeed a helplessness—it is only then that Moment I will have occurred; it is only then that the stage will have been set for the possibility of Moment II. So well understood is all this by specialists in this problem that, tragic as Moment I is in itself, in certain cases its coming about is devoutly hoped for. In fact, when the patient simply will not hit bottom, sometimes the bottom has to be brought up to the patient. For example, an employer may have to fire a man, or a wife to initiate divorce action, with the conscious purpose of forcing an awareness of his condition and its consequences. Nowadays experiments are being made in the use of drugs with a pseudo-schizophrenic effect, in order to crack the subject's vestige of false integration. More commonly, those closest to the subject simple wait until he reaches the end of his rope.

Is something like this necessary? Is desperation a precondition for entering the fullness of the Christian experience? If so, there would not be many Christians—in any era. While no man—Christian or otherwise—is an example of perfect integration, perfect peace and serenity, with an unclouded sense of being in eternal life, the fact is that there are many people whose structures of character are sturdy enough—whether from a sense of conformity, from self-discipline, from a steady reliance on God, or from enough reliances on contingent things (which they doubtless do not view as contingent), that they are far from a crack-up; they are nowhere near hitting bottom. Life may lack a certain luster, there may be trouble from time to time with various forms of anxiety, they may be seeking (intermittently or haphazardly, perhaps) something *more*, something deeper in life; but, in the large, it can be said that they are "all right." If all such people are excluded as candidates for Christianity, then it is doomed to being an esoteric religion indeed.

In fact, there has been a consistent tendency, reasserting itself throughout history in various forms, to achieve this very exclusiveness. The promoters of the early Gnostic heresy would limit the gift of the new life to the *illuminati*, those who were informed of and could grasp the *Gnosis*, the inner knowledge about reality. This heresy was formally condemned by the Church; but it has over and over again reflected itself in the movements and attitudes of those who believe themselves to be "in the know." Similar in its exclusiveness is mysticism. Here, not conceptual or intellectual knowledge, but direct apprehension of ultimate reality is seen as the key to the real life. This attitude has never been declared heretical, because it is capable of presentation in terms which are not exclusivist: namely, that this experience is not something essential, but is for some who are specially tuned in or who are specially called to it. But it has always been difficult for those devoted to this experience not to come to the attitude, actually more compatible with Oriental religions, that they have the real thing and that all others are spiritually unwashed. Not dissimilar is the ambivalence among those who practice glossolalia, or speaking with tongues, as was recognized by St. Paul when faced with this phenomenon in the early Church (I Cor. 12—14) and by some Church administrators today.[2]

---

[2] See, e.g., Pastoral Letter, Diocese of California, Third Sunday after Easter, 1963 (reprinted in *The Living Church*, May 19, 1963).

Another form of exclusivism has been a view held by most Christians in most centuries: man can be saved only by direct knowledge of Jesus Christ and explicit response to Him. Others have gone further, limiting salvation to the members of a particular denomination or to those who impliedly are members of it.[3] Persistent throughout Christian thought and belief has been an unvarnished "flat" doctrine of Predestination and Election (see Chap. VI), whereby God has selected specific individuals (generally conceived of as a minority) for salvation and eternal bliss, all others having been selected for eternal damnation.

So likewise for some (especially those connected with the more revivalistic sects or with revivalistic movements within the standard denominations), salvation is limited to those who have hit bottom first—who quite evidently, to judge from universal human experience, constitute a distinct minority in any time or place. This is obviously contrary to the preaching and practice of the Holy Catholic Church throughout the centuries. The incorporation of large masses of people into the Church in the early centuries (usually after the conversion of the king), though doubtless too indiscriminate—and often accompanied by a form of duress, is a witness against any such exclusivist view. An even more abiding witness is the practice of infant baptism. In each such service there is proclaimed the gift of salvation and eternal life; yet the recipients obviously have not experienced Moment I (the frequent occasion of their tears only superficially suggests a traumatic experience!) or Moment II—at least on the actual occasion itself (though when the baby smiles it is reassuring). Those denominations that have sought to make baptism an actual experience of Moment II (and to be preceded by some form of Moment I) generally end up not with adult believers' baptism but with delayed infant baptism, for those members of the family in their early teens are baptized as "adults" although they are

---

[3] E.g., for the Roman Catholic Church, people who are not consciously members of the Roman Catholic Church because of their "invincible ignorance" (subject to possible revision as a result of the Vatican Council).

really not mature enough for a decisive experience; in practice, they are selected on a basis of this norm: their "decision" is an expected thing for their age level (this is likewise generally true of Confirmation in Churches like my own which reserve this portion of the initiatory rite for a later conscious "decision").

It is true that from time to time adult baptism or confirmation may be the formal and public representation of the actual experience of the conversion of one who has reached the end of his rope in terms of meaning or conduct-pattern, and who has come to personal resurrection and new life. But we administer just the same sacraments—and in many more instances—to those for whom, from infancy upwards, this is not in fact the case.

William James's distinction between the once-born and the twice-born is valuable. But his conviction that genuine religious experience is limited to the latter—to those who utter an anguished cry for help—and is barred to the "healthy-minded," is really in radical conflict with main-line Christianity. And this in spite of the fact that the central experience of a Paul, an Augustine, a Luther, a St. Theresa, a John Bunyan, a George Fox, more or less matches what is the core of Christian belief—the great Moment I and the great Moment II. Christian practice has affirmed that a universal God has not been revealed in the scene of human history only in order that such, and their many (but, in terms of the whole population, relatively few) counterparts, might have fulfillment.

Does this mean that we must redefine Christiantiy as a philosophy—an ordered set of propositions—for the "healthy-minded," rather than as the proclamation of two great verbs which are more obviously congruent with the crucial experience of (to use William James's phrase) the "sick souls"? No, we can still center on the two great verbs and also include, equally, the healthy-minded within the ambit of salvation. And in doing so we do not water down the centrality of the two great Moments. In fact we enhance their significance in *breadth* while affirming their involvement with the Ultimate Depth. So ultimate and so cosmic are the

two great Moments that all men—whether twice-born or not—
may identify with them and have eternal life—now. *This identification is not merely in terms of belief in them and recognition
of their centrality in Christian faith, but in terms of actual sharing
in the depth and height of the once-and-for-all moments which
God has manifested—indeed lived out—in Jesus Christ.*

And that which the once-born thus enter is as genuinely the
new life as that which the twice-born can know. William James
describes the experience of the latter as "an altogether new level
of spiritual vitality, a relatively heroic level in which impossible
things have become possible and new energies and endurances are
shown." This can describe equally well the ongoing life of the
Christian whose faith and life is the product of Christian motivation, even though he may be less aware of the dimensions of his
existence and lack the personal sense of contrast between the old
life and the new—never having known vividly the emptiness of an
old life.

In connection with the twice-born we used two "case histories."
In contrast we present one of the "once-born"—one deliberately
designed to stand at the other extreme from a conscious "twice-
born" pattern (recognizing that many people fall somewhere in
between). A businessman was raised by nonchurchgoing parents
who, somewhat diffidently, subjected him to four or five years of
Sunday School—in which he learned how to make cut-outs and
was taught a few prudential moralisms associated with a pastel
Jesus, a somewhat precious man pictured in the materials. After
going through college and a graduate school of business administration, he centered his existence around a career in the managerial
class, around his family, and around an equable life in suburbia. A
persistently teasing sense of incompleteness became more and more
evident to him, but at no point did there dawn on him what James
describes (of himself) as "a horrible fear of my own existence,"
nor did he ever picture what the latter describes as "that pit of
insecurity beneath the surface of life." All the same, he was
open to an invitation of his next-door neighbor—and occasional

golfing companion—to join him and his wife in attending a preaching mission at the latter's church. He liked it: he reacted nostalgically (Sunday School had made some impression) to the Gospel hymns; the preacher's line made sense; and the coffee hour each night was almost as jolly as his customary daily cocktail party— the stimulus having come from the emotional lift which came from the hymn-sing, the standing-room-only crowd, and the preaching (which achieved "modified rapture").

So next Sunday he and his wife (she went along because she was worried about some other things, such as his relationship— obscure to her—to his secretary and his quietly incipient alcoholism: *anything* might help) accepted the neighbors' invitation to church—*cum* barbecue after; and it was all "nice": a dignified service, a sensible sermon and an equally good coffee hour. Before long he and his wife found themselves in an adult confirmation class (with "nice people"), and he was among them when the bishop arrived for the Laying on of Hands. On that day they were confirmed; the bishop said (and we can assume that the words— not absolutely, but representatively—reflect the Christian Faith): "Defend, O Lord, this thy child with thy heavenly grace, that he may *continue* thine forever, and daily increase in thy Holy Spirit *more and more* until he come into thy heavenly Kingdom." Nothing crucial about that. He eased in.

And yet what the bishop prayed for happened. He began to recognize (during the classes and after the sacramental rite) that he was and continued to be God's child and that more and more he was living in a larger context for inspiration. As he heard more and more, he "opened up" more and more, life was bigger for him, his energies increased and were directed with more discrimination. Central to all this was his knowing (not with bursting excitement to be sure) and indeed *appropriating*—in good part by osmosis—that the worst he had known (never with traumata in his case—stable he) or could know, had been endured by Jesus Christ, his very Confrere, and that it had all turned out all right— up to and beyond his largest measure of hopes (and his were not extravagantly large). His priority-scale was clearer, his decision-making a little more sure, his community attitudes a bit more creative. And maybe bigger things lay ahead: do you suppose he might someday even resign from the country club because of its long-standing segregation policy? (That this was not immediate does not provide a contrast with the twice-born: as Professor James has helped us to see, we cannot count on changes in specific attitudes or behavior from a conversion—St. Paul, unpleasant before his conversion, is still crochety in II Corinthians!).

Now this is not a glorious—or even particularly interesting—character. But there are many, many more of him than there are Pauls, Theresas, Bunyans—or for that matter, William Jameses. And they are *in* too. Why? Because all that is in Paul, Theresa, Bunyan, and James has permanently—and perennially—*happened* once and for all in Jesus Christ, who acted "for us and for our salvation." Our businessman (in the example above) has become part of that. And who knows what—in the various "changes and chances of this mortal life"—may be the whole outcome of the resulting "fruits of the Spirit"?

Let us visit a rural slum near a resort town in southern Mexico. No other Church (even the traditionally predominant one) is in there and so, by default, we are *the* Church—and our priest is the parson (etymologically, *the person*) there. Hence the eight hundred residents are divisible into members and sympathizers. Among both are some very simple folk—judged by U. S. standards —but those attending the Eucharist in Spanish, in a sort of dugout with the only light (except for the altar candles—in this use functional) coming from the oil lamps brought by the worshipers, join heartily in all the responses and choral portions of the service and listen with earnest expectation as, phrase by phrase, an English-speaking bishop's sermon is translated. These are certainly Christian; in a quite nonconceptual way their lives are bound up with the two great moments. And, in an immeasurable way, their lives are different from those who haven't "come 'round," but who, during that hour, just sit, with their tortillas, cigarros, and guitars.

God did it in Christ—once and for all, in a big way. Those for whom He has acted in personal, individual terms—knowing once and for all the down and the up—can "group" their individual experiences with that. But those without the latter experience are nevertheless a part of it. That is, to a degree; which is true too of the twice-born (remember Dr. James's careful modifier in the phrase, "a relatively heroic level").

What, then, is the nature of the incorporation of the once-born and the twice-born alike into the Great Twice-born Experience. It is that, putting their faith in it, it becomes for them an inspiration or an example? Yes, this certainly. By analogizing his own experience to the Great Analogue, the twice-born man attributes to his own conversion a more cosmic meaning and his personal integration is likely to be deepened, stabilized, and more abiding. And the once-born will find in the Cross comfort in his downs—some quite crucial—and in the Resurrection inspiration to be up again. But much more than this is involved, and while it is hard to express—and in any case is a mystery—the Church from the earliest days on has been at pains to seek to express it.

These are some of the ways:

1. It is asserted that by baptism the believer (the infant baptizee is putatively such) becomes actually part of *the body of Christ.* As St. Paul says, "Christ is like a single body with its many limbs and organs, which, many as they are, together make up one body. For indeed we were all brought into one body by baptism, in the one Spirit . . . Now you are Christ's body, and each of you a limb or organ of it" (I Cor. 12:12, 13, 27, NEB).

2. It is proclaimed that Christ is *in us* and that we are *in Him.* E.g., "Dwell in me, as I in you" (John 15:4); "I live; yet not I, but Christ liveth in me" (Gal. 2:20); ". . . that he may dwell in us and we in him."[4]

3. A related way of putting it is that the Spirit of Christ (or the Holy Spirit: in the New Testament the phrases are used alternatively) dwells in us.

4. The members of the Church are called, "the Bride of

[4] Book of Common Prayer, Canon of the Eucharist, p. 81; also see p. 82.

Christ"; marriage is seen as an analogy of "the mystical union [alternatively, "the spiritual marriage and unity"] which is betwixt Christ and His Church."[5]

5. The analogy of a plant is used: "I am the vine and you are the branches" (John 15:5).

6. We are typologically and archetypally identified with Adam in sin and death and with the second Adam, Jesus Christ, in new life. "For as in Adam all die, even so in Christ shall all be made alive" (I Cor. 15:22; see also Rom. 5:12-19); and "the man made of dust is the pattern of all men of dust, and the heavenly man is the pattern of all the heavenly. As we have worn the likeness of the man made of dust, so we shall wear the likeness of the heavenly man." (I Cor. 15:48-49). In his well-known hymn Cardinal Newman thus expressed the theme:

> O loving wisdom of our God!
> When all was sin and shame,
> A second Adam to the fight
> And to the rescue came.
> O wisest love! that flesh and blood,
> Which did in Adam fail,
> Should strive afresh against the foe,
> Should strive and should prevail.[6]

In these quotations we find the First Adam/Second Adam imagery used three ways: (a) we are actually *in* the two Adams; (b) they are the *patterns* of the down and the up of the individual; and (c) the second Adam acts for us and wins the victory for us. Oft repeated, of course, in the New Testament and other early Christian writings is the affirmation that in the Cross and Resurrection, God in Christ has definitely won the victory against sin.

7. Rather than identifying the down situation with the meaningful myth of the Fall of Man in Adam, and the up situation with

---

[5] Book of Common Prayer, pp. 300, 303; cf. Eph. 5:22-33.
[6] "Praise to the Holiest in the height," in, e.g., The [Episcopal] Hymnal 1940, Hymn 343.

our Lord's victory, another approach—more consistent with what has preceded—has been to identify both with Christ: the down with His death and the up with His resurrection. "Have you forgotten that when we were baptized into union with Christ Jesus we were baptized into his death? By baptism we were buried with him, and lay dead, in order that, as Christ was raised from the dead in the splendour of the Father, so also we might set our feet upon the new path of life" (Rom. 6:3-4, NEB).

Whichever way—and there are other ways—it is put (and none of these images is itself the ultimate truth), the basic reality sought to be represented is the possibility of a true *incorporation* of the individual, in the center of his existence, into God's involvement with the depth and height of human existence. This concept becomes particularly explicit in a new translation of Romans 6:5 (NEB): "For if we have become incorporate with him in a death like his, we shall also be one with him in a resurrection like his."

Faith (and personal decision based on that faith) in this reality involves two premises. Both are hard to state and unprovable; but neither is incredible or implausible—in fact both are plausible. They are:

1. *The basic solidarity of the human race.* As we shall see in the consideration of Original Sin,[7] it is not just a doctrine, but a plain historical, sociological, and psychological fact that evil—whether sin as such or anxiety patterns or any of the destructive aspects of life—is socially conditioned and has societal effects. As John Donne reminded us, "No man is an islande, intire of it selfe." And just as this is true of evil, it is true of good—and of the good life. This is far from an adequate analogy to the individual's incorporation into the mighty acts of God in Christ. But a depressed, cynical, and wrongly-motivated member of a family, or one whom circumstances have downed, can drag down those incorporated with him in this human unit. Likewise, the conversion of one such into a joyous, victorious person can elate—

[7] See Chap. VI.

indeed bring new life (perhaps even conversion) to others in the family.

The same is true of other human groupings, small and large. A member of a gang, or a church, or a club, or a faculty can be the avenue of evil or good to others in the corporation. The demonic possession of a Hitler can possess millions in a nation; the buoyant courage of a Churchill can give sustained hope and strength to his fellow citizens. More than this, the effects of men of either type—or in either situation—are much more widespread than the limits of their own group, much more widespread than is calculable. And not only upon their contemporaries: the actual lives, attitudes, and situations of men in subsequent history can be dynamically affected by the personality and decisions of a single man, who has thus become part and parcel of many lives. Here there is, in a measure at least, true incorporation.

While any such examples are inadequate to communicate the import of the human solidarity premise of incorporation in the crucial break-through of God in Christ, they do indicate that the latter premise is not simply something out of the blue; there is an empirical basis for its plausibility.

2. *The solidarity of God and man.* Here we do not mean a simple identification of God and man in either the pantheistic sense or as would be affirmed in hyper-mysticism or by the "new thought" cults. In the biblical tradition, there is always a *remove* between God and man, not only in terms of being but in terms of purpose (". . . neither are your ways my ways, says the Lord."[8]), knowledge ("Touching the Almighty, we cannot find him out"[9]) and relationship; each of us is a relatively free center of individual autonomy, in varying degrees of connection with life and with God and His aims.

Yet, as is suggested by the biblical affirmation that man is made in the image of God, there is a correlation between the dynamics of man's genuine fulfillment and God's own nature and activity. The thirst for new life is typical of men made aware of the

[8] Isa. 55:8.
[9] Job 37:23.

inadequacy of the life of "the old Adam"; if the more explicit version of conversion to new life lies in the experience of the twice-born, then the explicit demonstration in history of the cosmic prototype of this perennial human experience need not be seen as incredible and as quixotic, but as plausible and as *expected* (as indeed it was, in the Suffering Servant strain[10] of the Hebrew messianic tradition). We will be considering later[11] how we should—and should not—conceive of God; but it can be said now that the view of God as the Ultimate Ground of all being (rather than the conventional picture of Somebody "up there"— a Being beside other beings) builds up rather than tears down the plausibility of the ultimacy of the Great Moments I and II.

Experience shows that the most reliable way of persistently re- membering the crucial down and up in personal life is through participation in a group identifying with what otherwise would seem to be isolated and lonely experiences. In this Alcoholics Anonymous and other problem-centered groups, while using a minimum of ecclesiastical words, are manifestations of the latent Church in the world. More like the New Testament churches in this regard than typical present-day parishes are, they provide a vivid (though partial) image of what the Church is supposed to be. Except in one-to-one relationships (e.g., with the pastor) there is little explicit sharing of the individual down and up or identification with one another in it—and with the Great Mo- ments I and II. Yet this identification is implicit in the fact that the Church is the Body of Christ, and is meant to be explicit in the two Sacraments in which all this is continually celebrated.[12] Out of this should stem *love* of one another and *mission* to the world.

[10] See, principally, Isa. 52:13—53:12.
[11] See Chap. VII.
[12] In, e.g., Anglican services, the baptized person "with the residue of thy holy Church" is declared to be "buried with Christ in his death" and made a "partaker of his resurrection," and in the Eucharist "we and all thy whole Church" identify through "having in remembrance his blessed passion and precious death, his mighty resurrection" (Book of Common Prayer, pp. 281, 81).

VI: GOOD OUT OF EVIL

MOMENT I—whether it be the Great Moment I of Christ's Passion and death or the various—and varied—Moments I in the experience of countless individuals—is in itself a bad thing. Resurrection or no, the imposition of a cruel form of capital punishment upon the most guileless One we have ever known, the doing to death of this utterly honest and courageous One by evil conspirators, is unmitigated evil. Too, an individual's loss of a living and vital faith is in itself a misfortune, whether or not for such a person there is a later Moment II—enabling him to go through the paces of life with a larger dimension of meaning. And a spirit debilitated by overwhelming ennui is in a bad way, whether or not the lack of a Moment II dooms the rest of his days to cynicism and tastelessness. An alcoholic's actual hitting bottom is pitiful in itself, and when there is no Moment II, the initial tragedy may be followed by repeated tragedies of the same genre. And to go beyond the type of Moment I where most of those suffering it represent part or all of the cause of their own pit experience (as in the case of the various examples in the previous chapter), there are many instances of sheer hurt and tragedy where—with or without a Moment II—the causes appear to be principally or totally due to others or to nonhuman and impersonal forces.

No person passes many years without experiencing evil or having been the object of its impact, in one or another of its various forms. The depth and breadth of the experience of such a particular event bears on whether or not there has really been a Moment I, i.e., the first step in what can become a twice-born experience. In any case these experiences are part of the fundamental reality of faith in, and incorporation into, the Great Moments I and II—important for the once-born as well as for the twice-born. So it depends on how we understand evil and where we go from there, whether we can go "beyond tragedy" (to use the title of one of Reinhold Niebuhr's books). First, then, we must explore the nature of evil in relation to God's purposes, and next ask ourselves the question: Where can we go from there—with God? We will undertake these two steps of analysis in reference to two fairly distinguishable types of evil: the evil the individual himself appears to have decided to do—what is commonly called "sin"; and evil where the cause appears to be outside of the individual. (It is with the second connotation that the word "evil" is used in the narrower sense, as in the phrase "the problem of evil," and we shall so use it throughout the rest of this chapter.) In short, evil and sin.

EVIL

As old as philosophy and theology itself is the problem of evil. Why does evil exist? What is its source? This is not merely an intellectual question: a quite untutored woman confronted with the accidental death of her husband can cry out, "How could a good God allow such a thing to happen?" The fact is that unexplained evil in the world is a persistent roadblock to faith. People of a wide range of intellectual naïveté and sophistication find an apparent inconsistency between the claim that God is all-good and the claim that God is all-powerful. Public opinion will readily support the courts in acquitting a defendant who has lost control of his automobile, since a man is not expected to be in perfect control of all the factors surrounding his existence; but people who are hurt do not so easily clear God of responsibility for damaging factors not of their own making and choosing. For they have been taught that He is omnipotent, i.e., able to make things run right; and obviously things have not run right.

A fairly conclusive solution of the paradox can be stated as to a very large category of evils suffered by individuals, namely, those brought about, directly or indirectly, by their own decisions or by those of other human beings.

One of the most significant characteristics of man is his freedom. It is true that man is not as free as heretofore generally thought; an increasingly profound anthropological, sociological, and psychological knowledge of man's condition makes clearer and clearer that the area of free decision-making is considerably hedged in. Yet almost universally experienced in the very act of decision-making is the intuition which supports the conclusion (which in turn rests on faith) that most men most of the time are free to make certain decisions among alternatives. As the late French scientist Lecomte du Noüy reminded us, man is the first being evolved who henceforth would be in on the evolving. We do have a hand in things and hence are generally responsible for the decisions we make. A necessary corollary is that not only is man free to do good and constructive things but he is also free to do evil and destructive things. In our unhappiness about having experienced the fact of the latter half of the corollary, we can fault God, if we wish, for permitting human freedom; but we cannot fault Him for the fact that human freedom, once evolved, necessarily implies the possibility that a person's decisions may hurt himself or another, and that the decisions of whole groups of people may hurt a single person or whole groups.

This logic obviously applies to direct harm from a free decision: if in connection with a bank hold-up the thief decides that it is safer for him to kill the teller, this death, no matter how tragically the result is viewed, raises no problem about either the goodness or the omnipotence of God. And the same is true of the tragic result of an unfree action that is corollary to a free decision: if a drunken driver crashes into another car and seriously injures someone, it may be true that he lacked the freedom to do otherwise at the time of the accident—due to his desensitized condition; but he was free (assuming that he is not a compulsive alcoholic) to drink or not to drink or to regulate or not to regulate the quantity of his intake. A man weighing 250 pounds may die of a heart attack at 55 not because of any decision he made at the time of his death, but because of a whole series of little decisions made at meals thrice a day for a number of years before his death.

Much evil can be attributed to social conditioning involving the decisions of a number—perhaps a very large number—of people, maybe over many generations. It is commonplace to attribute juvenile delinquency to poor home conditions, which presumably involve the individual decisions of parents; yet we can refer (totally or in part) the causation of their decisions to defects in economic and educational systems; and we can in turn refer much of this blame to the wrong exercise (or nonexercise) of freedom on the part of multitudes of people over a number of generations.

The same is possibly true as to the cause of a variety of disorders generally regarded as impersonal. For example, one speculative theory about the origins of cancer is that the human system is simply not geared to the enormous pressures and speed of modern life. Just as a model-T Ford I once owned used to rattle and shake when I tried to drive it too fast up a hill since it was simply not made for that kind of achievement, so too in these hectic days there occurs in certain individuals that erraticism called cancer. This particular theory may not prove to be valid; but it is suggestive of the fact that some of the serious illnesses which we would normally tend to attribute only to physical causes may have their origin in deleterious factors in our society, which in turn are rooted in human decision-making—though of course not necessarily in wrong decisions of the particular people afflicted. Apart from the extreme example just used, psychosomatic medicine is able to attribute more and more physical illness to mental disposition; and some factors at least of the latter lie within the realm of free human choice.

While, then, we should recognize that the scope of the evils that we can attribute, in whole or in part, to man's actions or attitudes is wider than had heretofore been generally acknowledged, the fact remains that the exercise of man's freedom by no means encompasses the whole range of evil in our world. There is the familiar story of the merchant planning with an insurance agent a program of coverage for his new store. He had signed up for fire and theft insurance and when asked to extend the coverage to tornado damage, retorted, "Can I start a tornado?" By no stretch of imagination can we attribute to man and his freedom the causing of a hurricane which kills or injures thousands and leaves many other thousands homeless.

To turn to a quite different field, we have learned, often too late, that deforestation, by man's decision (whether stupid or selfish) can affect the availability of water in an area to man's hurt. And we know that when farmers fail to rotate crops or to allow the land to lie fallow they leave the soil relatively unfit for agricultural production—to man's hurt. But a man's being struck by lightning can seldom be attributed to his error in judgment, or to that of any other man. Not entirely specious is the labeling of such an event as an "act of God." In the sense in which this phrase is commonly used in the Anglo-Saxon law, it means that the event is in nowise an act caused by man; but the wording rests on the implied premise that God alone is the cause. If the premise were made explicit, it would be affirmed that God decided to make it happen. In fact, in the more primitive view of the biblical faith this was a fairly common assumption—or even affirmation—as to public disasters and private ones. There are a good number of examples in the Old Testament (e.g., the Flood, the destruction of Sodom and Gomorrah, the striking down of individuals) and even in the New Testament (e.g., the deaths of Ananias and Sapphira reported in Acts 5).

As far as death from such causes goes it can be said that this is not a *special* evil, in that all men will die sometime anyway, and hence in particular deaths at a given time no special problem is raised about God's goodness and/or omnipotence; the real problem is: why does He allow death at all? And if we are not prepared to say that death is necessarily an evil, especially in the light of belief in eternal life, we need not here speculate further in this direction. But whatever view we might take about the relationship between death and evil, lifelong crippling injuries or even those of shorter duration, or homelessness and starvation, are incontrovertibly evil in themselves.

When we have narrowed the area as much as possible, eliminating all categories where human freedom could possibly be involved either directly or indirectly, either individually or corporately, and have eliminated the category of death on the assumption that it is not necessarily bad, nevertheless the problem of evil still remains in its hard-core form.

What are the possible explanations?

1. There are two Gods, one whose purposes are good and beneficent and one whose purposes are evil and malevolent. This is the solution offered by Zoroastrianism and by Manicheanism in early Christian history. Such a conviction would have to rest on faith just as does the conviction that there is only one God; and it would seem to be a less plausible faith in that it would deny the possibility of a *universe*—a premise basic to the scientific method no less than to the perennial philosophical and theological enterprise.

2. There is one God; but operating in the world—by his leave, as it were—is a created and rebellious evil being with forces at his command which can affect the spiritual and material order. This theory, centered around the Devil and his host of fallen angels, has been a persistent one within the Judeo-Christian tradition.

Now as we shall see, the "demonic" is a useful category in picturing the configuration of reality (or, better, the disfiguration of reality) as the context in which individual sin and evil-doing can be better understood. But a literal belief in the Devil does not absolve God on the problem of evil: it simply adds to the problem.

Why does He allow this great evil to exist and to function destructively alongside His own constructive activity? Conversely, we certainly have no way of knowing enough about reality to affirm that there are no free beings in the universe other than man: while we certainly cannot prove the existence of angels, we cannot disprove their existence either. And if there is such a category of beings and if freedom has been granted to them, as it has to man, then we need not necessarily attribute to God such evils as the free decision of such beings may bring about. But in the case of man who has freedom, we do have some empirical experience on which to base our faith, whereas in the case of angels or devils we have absolutely nothing to go on as a basis for faith in them—except supposition expressed in Scriptures, in the writings of certain theologians, and in widespread popular belief. As we have indicated in Chapter I, plausibility is an important element in faith; and there does not seem to be a great deal of plausibility here, the late C. S. Lewis in *The Screwtape Letters* to the contrary notwithstanding.

3. A more far-reaching variant of the above theory is this: the factor of freedom exists not only in man (and possibly in angels) but in all of nature, from the simplest atom all the way up to the most complex organisms. Proponents of this theory extend the mythological concept of the Fall of Man (pp. 96f.) to the Fall of all Creation, i.e., evil motivation exists along with constructive purpose in the physical order. This too has some, if sparse, biblical basis (e.g., "the whole creation groaneth and travaileth in pain together until now" [Rom. 8:22, KJV]).

But if we assume that the respective elements of the material order are operating in this ambivalent way without an inherent individual consciousness prerequisite to decision-making, God Himself (or an independent God of evil or a Devil) is still left as being the source of evil. On the other hand, to presuppose self-consciousness in matter has no empirical basis.

4. There is only one God, but His motives are a mixture of good and evil, as in the case of men. This too would seem to be

less plausible than belief in a God who is all-good, since the revelations of God we have known in the most significant areas of meaning have shown grace and goodness, principally in the life, teaching, sacrificial death, and victorious resurrection of Jesus Christ. Further, our characteristic response of worship to Him as Absolute, as "the Most High," rests on the presupposition that He is unadulterated Goodness. While this act of faith is not disproof of the theory, it does detract from its plausibility, on the ground of incongruity.

5. Like the above theory in end result is a flat view of the doctrine of Predestination: before all worlds certain men yet to be created (and the proponents of this view—indicate that this means relatively few) have been elected to salvation and are predestined, willy-nilly, to eternal bliss, while the rest of mankind has been predestined to eternal damnation. It has been asserted further that good things in this life for the elect (and evil things for the damned) are the predestined fruitage of their unearned status before God. As Max Weber pointed out, this conviction provided an effective ideological basis for the development of capitalism in the West. (Regardless of the truth of the doctrine there is certainly a psychological basis for Weber's theory: a belief that one is of the elect certainly would contribute to his self-confidence and sense of rightness in the possession of good things —and would also engender patience about their own penury on the part of those lacking the sense of eternal election.)

But what this doctrine really comes down to in the end is that God deliberately and effectively wills an evil outcome for the mass of mankind, and hence while He is omnipotent, He is not all-good. Nor, incidentally, under the extrapolation of the "double predestination" theory, are the elect in heaven really *good* in their supposed joy in observing the sufferings of the damned.

6. There is one God, and He is good; but He is not omnipotent. He would like things to go better, but He is not quite on top of them. This view can be conceived of in a number of ways: (*a*) God never was and never will be omnipotent; (*b*) God Himself

is part of the evolutionary process and has not yet fully evolved into absolute power (this is a rough-and-ready summary of Whitehead's concept of God as part of the evolving universe rather than "an all-foreseeing Creator," creation seen as being a continuing process and the process being viewed as itself *the* actuality); (c) in the evolution of matter God's dynamic energy is confronted with a high degree of inertness and turgidity in the material universe and it takes time to shape things up.

But (a) is totally inconsistent with the unifying concept of God as the Ultimate Ground of all Being; it leaves Him simply as a being beside other beings (albeit one considerably more powerful than, e.g., a strong man), the difference being only one of degree rather than of quality. This is a less plausible view of God than the view of Him as the Ultimate Ground. While (b) and (c) would imply some evident progress in the ordering of the universe (apart, of course, from humanly initiated projects), such progress is not at all empirically evident. Are hurricanes and earthquakes less frequent or less disastrous than in centuries or millennia gone by? On the other hand, the appearance of rational and co-creative beings as well as of the higher forms of animal life does seem to indicate that new *means* of ordering have appeared in the course of time. Yet at the same time human beings (also animals) are causes of new evils.

7. There is one God, He is omnipotent and basically good; but He literally brings evil upon us to punish us. Although there is considerable biblical precedent for this theory, it is implausible for a number of reasons: (a) the degree of evil often would seem to be disproportionate to the offense (and we would expect God to be at least as just in this regard as are the criminal courts when informed by sound penology); (b) there is no obvious correlation between the sinners and the recipients of evil (Jesus pointed this out when asked whether or not a man's blindness was due to his own sin or that of his father. His answer was neither [John 9:3]); (c) as to the mode of punishment, good parents seek to provide deprivations (excluding deprivations which cause harm to health)

rather than positive injury to their children as punishments; again we would expect God to do at least as well.

8. There is but one God, He is omnipotent and basically good; but he deliberately brings evil upon us to test us and to develop faith and trust toward Him. This, too, has a biblical basis, e.g., "My son, despise not thou the chastening of the Lord, nor faint when thou art rebuked of him: For whom the Lord loveth he chasteneth, and scourgeth every son whom he receiveth" (Heb. 12:5-6, RSV); and it is also reflected in later writings, e.g., the Book of Common Prayer. For example, a Collect for the Communion of the Sick reads:

Almighty, everliving God, Maker of mankind, who dost correct those whom thou dost love, and chastise every one whom thou dost receive; We beseech thee to have mercy upon this thy servant visited with thine hand, and to grant that he may take his sickness patiently, and recover his bodily health, if it be thy gracious will. . . ."[1]

Again, we expect more of God than of a good parent, and while an earthly father would hope that his child would have the strength to bear up under strain, he would not deliberately inflict pain in order to test his child as to whether he can "take it" and will still love and trust his father without qualification. God's approach is not to be reduced to the tactics of the pledge-master during a fraternity hell-week!

From a logical point of view, the above eight possibilities would seem to represent about the only possibilities. There may be others; but it is apparent that no one of the above provides an adequate, congruent, or convincing answer to the problem of evil. The fact is that neither the philosophers nor the theologians have provided a satisfactory answer to this basic question. Nevertheless we do not remain helpless on this account; the experience with God as known in the Judeo-Christian tradition, based on, or resulting in, faith in Him, has provided us with a dynamic for dealing with the fact

[1] P. 321.

of evil. We can distinguish the aspects of the problem by recalling the familiar prayer, falsely but reverently attributed to Reinhold Niebuhr: "God grant me the serenity to accept things I cannot change, courage to change things I can, and wisdom to know the difference."

What is represented by the first two clauses in this prayer came from the Judeo-Christian tradition into Western culture as a tremendous dynamic to look realistically at *what is*, and to seek to repair whatever is evil or incomplete. A key text in this regard is St. Paul's dictum: "And be not conformed to this world; but be ye transformed . . ., that ye may prove what is that good, and acceptable, and perfect will of God" (Rom. 12:2, KJV). Christians, at their best, do not simply regard themselves as a committee seeking particular moral reforms. They regard themselves as citizens in another dimension of reality which permeates the present and the forever: in the New Testament called the Kingdom of God. Secure in this eternal relationship, they have the courage and resources to maintain as to the earthly scene both detachment and involvement, i.e., the role of "colonists." Colonialism (not a very popular idea today) traditionally has sought to make the strange place approximate the homeland, in this case what St. Thomas Aquinas has called "our true native land."

In his work of colonization the colonist is not just striking out in the dark; he already has a blueprint of the ideal, namely, the patterns of life and culture in his homeland. As uncritical as colonists have been of this image—particularly with regard to the appropriateness of its transplantation into a wholly different area with a different historical social conditioning—this process does provide an analogy for the outlook and dynamic of the Christian in his reaction to the world around him. He believes in the reality of God's realm, though it is far from fully manifest on the earthly scene. He believes that it will be manifested in God's own time. Thus his activities toward its realization in more and more situations here and now are supported not only by hope as to short-range achievements but by faith in the complete manifestation.

This faith is generally expressed in the image of the Second Coming, wherein the truth and goodness which have been perceived "in the time of this mortal life" in which He was known to us in Jesus Christ "in great humility" will be seen as fully vindicated as the complete manifestation of this same Truth and Goodness, i.e., "in his glorious majesty," judging "the quick and the dead."[2] Thus the future fuels the present. Concern with final things (eschatology) has not only to do with some other world (giving the humanist ground for his taunt, "one world at a time"); it has to do with this world, with power for action now.

This conviction can manifest itself in terms of witness to the truth against the apparently insuperable odds of society, e.g., the boldness of the Maccabees and the courage of St. Stephen, the first Christian martyr, and of the early Christians thrown to the lions. In Church history after Constantine (especially when the Church had succeeded and had been established as part of the secular society) there has been a vacillation between sprinkling holy water on the status quo and a vigorous disturbance of the status quo. In the news today, the Church is most conspicuous in its allegiance to the Kingdom in unpopular efforts for social reform and opposition to segregation and other infringements of civil and religious liberty.

The work of the Kingdom is also operating as a leaven within society in the less controversial areas of improved social welfare. Behind all religiously motivated efforts to eradicate or ameliorate evil in human relations is the contrast between the *ought* of the pattern of the Kingdom and the *is* of the terrestrial scene.

The same dynamic has manifested itself in Western culture in less socially oriented but equally important research in physics, chemistry, biology, and medicine toward the eradication or prevention of inadequacies or disasters with end results in human life. Mechanics and technology play their part in implementing these aims. Representing the same drive too are corporate effort,

---

[2] The phrases quoted are from the Collect for Advent, Book of Common Prayer.

such as the development of low-cost, multiple-unit housing, planned parenthood clinics, reform of administrative machinery—in business, state, and Church—to get more done with less, development of better schools, the increase in the opportunities of healing, through clinics and through group therapy. Included is everything from the improvement of plumbing to the damming up of restless water to provide irrigation and electric power. Behind this whole enterprise, which has especially marked Western civilization, has been the conviction—often inarticulate—that we have an allegiance to an order of Good and that it is our responsibility to conform the existential situation to this order by sharing with God in the finishing of the creation and redemption of the world, in the turning of chaos (including the chaos which men in their freedom have made out of already existing order) into order. Granted that a lot of people who do not regard themselves as religious are also engaged in these tasks (sometimes more notably so than the pious). Yet the presence of this dynamic in Western culture clearly has a theological source, and it is not surprising that many who do not acknowledge this source are caught up in its power.

So the first Christian reaction to evil is to try to get rid of it and thus reduce the problem to whatever degree possible.

But there is plenty we have not got rid of. However complete the tidying up may eventually be, we must live in the interim. And Christianity has something to say as to this too. Consciousness of being geared into the Ultimate Ground of Being, openness to the strength and joy and grace of His Presence, has enabled many boxed in by evil to survive in joy. In fact, special talents are sharpened by the confinement. From, and in relation to, conditions in themselves evil, startling creativity and unique occasions of love have over and over been manifested in specific moments and patterns of individual personal life. Tragedy has engendered an openness to what is, and has made many men honest and without illusions, sharpened discernment as between what can be successfully worked out and what must be accepted and used and operated within. Persons who have known this strength and power within distressing limitations have come to greater involvement with the Ultimate Ground of their—and all—being. They have become more open to Him, enabling Him to share with them His security. They can then see their present situation in an eternal frame of reference, be possessed by the conviction that they are already in eternal life. And from this can come not only power for good out of evil now, but also the comfort that that which is not right here will be made right for what is by far the longer period in one's life—this life being the tiniest fragment of all of one's life as an individual personality, which is forever and ever. Thus assured, one can experience the fact that the meaning of eternity can be manifested now, enjoyed now, and be a source of power and effectiveness now.

This reality, received by faith, does not depend on dates or particular persons. But this faith, through experience, has come to Christians throughout the centuries principally through the central image of the break-through of strength and power through evil and suffering, namely, the Cross of Jesus Christ. He was boxed in: unjustly judged, hated, tortured, confined; yet from so few hours of a single man's life has come the greatest power and strength for all generations. This possibility of realization is the meaning of the Suffering Servant passages in the Book of Isaiah (52:13—53:12), and the meaning of the words reported as having been uttered by Christ from the Cross.[3] The vindication of this experience is the Resurrection, an assurance for all of us that we can be citizens of the eternal Kingdom, here and now operative and forever fulfilling.

Thus concerning evil, Christianity has little to say conclusively as to the *why*, but a great deal to say as to what to do about it and within it and beyond it.

Sin

As we have just seen, the scope of evils possibly attributable to God can be considerably narrowed, enabling us to focus on the hard-core problem of evil. The same is true as to the scope of

[3] See more fully my *Beyond Anxiety* (New York: Charles Scribner's Sons), Chap. IV.

wrongs apparently attributable to man. Similarly, analysis will narrow the scope of sins and thus reveal the true problem of sin.

Not every human act that results in unpleasant circumstances is a sin; not even every human evil intention (whatever the results) connotes sin. The fact is it is not as easy to sin as has been popularly supposed.

At the least, sin involves the wrong exercise of choice. With some persons at all times, and with all persons at some time, there is no freedom of choice. Due to sociological and psychological conditioning, a given person at a given time may be driven by compulsions arising from the repository of the unconscious mind. As is more and more recognized with the increase of psychiatric knowledge and experience, this is true of a considerable amount of homosexual behavior, and of the grosser acts of cruelty—even murder. A number of Churches (including the Roman and Anglican Communions) traditionally have denied Christian burial to those who have committed suicide. For example, a rubric at the beginning of the Church of England Order for the Burial of the Dead reads, "Here is to be noted, that the Office ensuing is not to be used for any that . . . have laid violent hands upon themselves. . . ."[4] But in practice the burial service *is* used for those who have taken their own lives. Why? Simply because now (due to greater psychological understanding) it is *assumed* that a person who has taken his own life has not done so freely, but rather due to a compulsion. In thus leaning over backward in favor of the deceased, it is assumed that Almighty God has the resources to endure the indignity of the use of the Christian service for one who, perchance, may have acted in complete freedom.

Here we have seen greater progress than in the field of criminal law. Whereas McNaughton's Case[5] withdrew criminal liability from persons who did not know the difference between right and wrong, the tendency now in the field of criminal law is to

[4] The American Prayer Book has been modified to read, "It is to be noted that this Office is appropriate to be used only for the faithful departed in Christ . . ." (p. 337).
[5] 10 C. L. & F. 200 (1843).

recognize that many persons who know the difference (including, perhaps, a professor of Christian ethics) may still be *incapable* of doing right and avoiding wrong because of genuine psychological compulsion. Moreover, the crime of "attempted suicide" is now used only as a practical device to confine and (hopefully) provide therapeutic help for unsuccessful attempters. Similarly, as far as sin goes, that which in times past was regarded as an attempt to commit the gravest of sins, namely, the taking of one's own life (it being assumed that since there was no opportunity to repent, the person was surely damned), existentially is no longer regarded as a sin, but simply as an important occasion for pastoral (and when available, psychiatric) counseling.

Sin presupposes freedom; and there is obviously considerably less freedom than our forefathers thought. Even for people without psychoses and with little neurosis (all of us are somewhat neurotic), conditioning and a measure of compulsion enter into decision-making even where it would appear that there is also a measure of freedom. Thus the degree to which a given act (or omission) is sinful is determined not only by the definition of the act but also by the relative proportions of freedom and compulsion in each instance. And not even the most proficient psychiatrist, let alone one's next-door neighbor, can measure this. Thus, appropriate is Jesus' injunction to "judge not." Nor can one measure this proportion in one's own actions. Thus to the point are St. Paul's words, "I judge not mine own self. For I know nothing by myself; yet am I not hereby justified: but he that judgeth me is the Lord" (I Cor. 4:3, 4, KJV). There is only One "unto whom all hearts are open, all desires known, and from whom no secrets are hid."[6]

These considerations are not meant to minimize sin. In fact the scope of possible sin is much wider than is generally appreciated by those who tend to be most confidently judgmental in regard to particular sins. Those, for example, of the pietistic tradition who with psychological naïveté categorize the problem of alcohol

---

[6] Eighth-century Collect: see Book of Common Prayer, p. 67.

simply in terms of sin (one drink is one sin, two drinks are two sins, *ad infinitum*—or rather, *ad finitum!*) are least likely to see sin involved at all in collaboration in patterns of racial segregation or just plain hard-nosed coldness to individuals they don't like. The realm of sin is as broad as the realm of human existence; life, in its personal, interpersonal, and societal aspects is under claim and hence under judgment.

The law is no less than total goodness in every action or called-for action, in the light of the capacities, opportunities, and confrontations of each individual—because God who is the Basis of the claim is the Source of the all with which an individual can, to a degree, meet it. There is only one of Him, hence He can claim all. The *Sh'ma Israel* has put things in the right order: "Hear, O Israel, the Lord thy God is one. And thou shalt love the Lord Thy God with all thy heart, with all thy mind, with all thy soul and with all thy strength." This is not some rule God has made up (as has been supposed to be the case with the various relative Commandments—which, generally speaking, express applications of this total claim to particular areas of decision-making). Rather, it is the expression of a necessary, final, and unchanging corollary to the fact of a God who is not just one thing among others in the world but is the Basis of all reality. Hence the claim is total both as to scope and as to degree of performance. "Be ye therefore perfect," our Lord said, "even as your Father which is in heaven is perfect" (Matt. 5:48, KJV).

As to the *application* of the Claim, sins differ *objectively* in degree of gravity. A citizen leading a movement to maintain segregation in housing is involved, as far as the character of the acts are concerned, in a much greater sin than is, for example, a man who is unreasonably hostile to his wife. The number of persons likely to be hurt in the first instance is greater and the duration of the hurt will doubtless be longer. Hence the first is worse than the second. However, *subjectively* (and, as has been said, only God knows the answer here) the husband's sin may be much greater than the segregationist's. Suppose that the given man's psychological make-up was sufficiently stable and his marriage sufficiently a going concern, that he acted with a high proportion of freedom; and suppose that the segregationist was not only beleaguered with personal prejudice but conditioned to rationalization of his position by his upbringing and by the actions of his group (and, as could be, his presuppositions have escaped challenge by his pastor's preaching or by the educational program of his parish). Though his action is more evil, *he* may be less sinful than the other man.

Since existentially there is such relativity as to the sinfulness, or degree thereof, of specific acts and attitudes, and since no one (save God)—even the "sinner"—can conclusively judge, confession of *sin* is more honest than confession of *sins*.

Many denigrate a "general confession" in a service of worship, as compared with conventional "private confession," on the ground that the former does not get down to particular sins. It is true that private confession to a wise pastor, by bringing out particular acts and patterns, can give a basis for practical help in reform and can help the penitent to give conscientious attention to particular aspects of undesirable behavior. Hence it is regrettable that more persons do not take advantage of this opportunity (and it is an opportunity available in all traditions, assuming a responsible pastor, not only in Churches that make explicit provision for the opportunity of private confession[7]). On the other hand, a judgment as to the quantity of actual guilt involved in a given sin (as reflected in a mechanical assignment of graduated penances) can be made by neither confessor nor penitent. Hence the relevance of general confession: *None* of us—pastor or layman—is inaccurate if we say ". . . we have not done those things we ought to have done, we have done those things we ought not to have done and there is no health [i.e., wholeness, perfect integration, purity of motive, and unqualified freedom to choose the good] in us."[8] And

---

[7] Cf. Book of Common Prayer, pp. 87-88, 313.
[8] The General Confession in the Daily Offices, Book of Common Prayer, pp. 6, 23-24.

for many at times in life, these words are not extravagant: "though we be tied and bound by the chains of our sins."[9] Herein we affirm the fact of sin which (excluding those unfortunate persons who are totally in the grip of conditioning and the projection of unconscious urges) embraces every last one of us—each in an utterly unique configuration. General Confession is descriptive in this regard and also in the corporate sense of the word: as human beings we are interlocked in sin.

This is the meaning of the doctrine of Original Sin and its picturization in the Edenic myth (cf. Gen. 1:26 ff.) The claim is there (subdue the earth), the freedom to act appropriately is there (Adam walked and talked with God), and the choice is put (the apple tree is there), and self-centeredness is there (and the serpent said to Eve, "ye shall be as gods"). Thus man is psychologically and sociologically conditioned from birth—and before. . . . "in[to[10]] sin did my mother conceive me" (Ps. 51:5). As the late Archbishop William Temple put it:

When we open our eyes as babies we see the world stretching out around us; we are in the middle of it; all proportions and perspectives in what we see are determined by the relation—distance, height, and so forth—of the various visible objects to ourselves. This will remain true of our bodily vision as long as we live. I am the centre of the world I see; where the horizon is depends on where I stand. Now just the same thing is true at first of our mental and spiritual vision. Some things hurt us; we hope they will not happen again; we call them bad. Some things please us; we hope they will happen again; we call them good. Our standard of value is the way things affect ourselves. So each of us takes his place in the centre of his own world. But I am not the centre of the world, or the standard of reference as between good and bad; I am not, and God is. In other words, from the beginning I put myself in God's place. This is my original sin. I was doing it before I could speak, and everyone else has been doing it from early infancy. I am not "guilty" on this account because I could not

---

[9] From the Penitential Office, Book of Common Prayer, p. 63.

[10] The distinction between "in" and "into" is not precise in any language; but in any case the "in" meaning is intolerable.

help it. But I am in a state, from birth, in which I shall bring disaster on myself and everyone affected by my conduct unless I can escape from it.[11]

Thus an individual sin is in part due to those factors we embrace under the title "Original Sin" and also adds to the force of Original Sin. Such is human solidarity in sin, as well as in redemption (pp. 75f.). When one says, "I don't believe in Original Sin," he may well be commended if he means that he rejects the negative view of human sexuality typical of most of Christian history or rejects the notion that because "our first parents" ate an apple, God was angry at the whole human race. But to eliminate the whole category of interrelatedness in evil-doing, which the complex mythology of Original Sin represents, is simple naïveté— psychological, historical, and sociological, no less than theological.

This is all complex, and the Church lacks clear and complete understanding—as in the case of nonhuman evil. But, as we have seen in the latter case, we grasp a dimension *beyond sin* and can bring something to bear on it toward its reduction and toward greater goodness.

The same God who is the Claimant is the Acceptor of the unsuccessful claimee. When a man acknowledges that he has fallen short he has, *ipso facto,* opened himself—to the depths of his being (compulsions, social conditioning, and all)—to the ever present, ever ready grace (because free and unlimited) which God is. Thus he can accept himself—though unacceptable (whether in terms of objective evil or of subjective responsibility).[12] The natural grateful response to this Gift, once received and appropriated, is power for action, dynamic for goodness. Now we truly *want* to fulfill the Claim we ought to fulfill. This is toward the cleansing and the perfect love referred to in the Collect, which attributes to the Claimant as judge the only true assessment of each man's sin; the full text:

[11] *Christianity and Social Order* (London: Penguin, 1942), pp. 37-38.
[12] See more fully my *Beyond Anxiety* Chaps. II and III; *Doing the Truth* (Garden City, N.Y.: Doubleday and Co., 1955), Chap. VII; and *The Next Day* (Doubleday, 1957), Chap. III.

Almighty God, unto whom all hearts are open, all desires known, and from whom no secrets are hid; Cleanse the thoughts of our hearts by the inspiration of thy Holy Spirit, that we may perfectly love thee, and worthily magnify thy holy Name; through Christ our Lord. Amen. [13]

Thus "beyond sin," just as "beyond evil," we are joined with the cosmic down-and-up reality, the great Moment I and Moment II through which God in constancy is ready to relate to us. So gracious is He.

[13] See n. 6, above.

VII: GOD AND
THE PARTICULAR

THE CREDIBILITY of the ultimacy of the core Events on which Christianity rests depends upon how we conceive of the underlying Source of these Events, namely, *God*.

Two strains have run parallel in Christian thought:

1. God is immutable, unchanging, imperturbable, unconditional. With Him past, present, and future are all the same. The clear implication of this portrayal is that He does not change His mind, get a new idea, develop a new plan. From this it would also be implied that He is uninfluenced in attitude or action by the wishes, deeds, or petitions of men—or by anything whatsoever.

2. God, like a human being, is time and time again adjusting His feelings and actions in accordance with historical and personal events and in response to requests of, and fulfillment of conditions laid down by, human beings. He grows angry, and then He "repenteth himself of the evil" and decides not to destroy after all. He responds like the magistrate who gives in after being repeatedly pressed by the importunate widow (cf. Luke 18:1-8). He arranges for the rise and fall of particular nations. He works out a special "dated" plan for the redemption of mankind.

Which kind of God is He? If He is like the first (constant and never changing), then several great Christian affirmations would seem to go by the boards: for example (*a*) Judgment and Providence (His positive role in human history); (*b*) the efficacy of prayer and sacrament; and (*c*) the work of Redemption in Jesus Christ: the cosmic down-and-up. If He is as described in (2), the anthropomorphism is too great a strain on intelligent belief. This is indeed the "scandal of particularity." Why should one grant that there is, in addition to the persons and things which are empirically evident to us, an unseen Person-Force who sometimes decides to allay evil or promote good and sometimes does not; Who sometimes feels kindly toward given persons and groups and sometimes feels hostile toward them; Who sometimes heals and sometimes does not; Who sometimes seems inoperative and at other times is pressed into action?

Yet both understandings of God have been so prevalent that each is likely to be representative of truth. For what is central in Christianity—the death and Resurrection of Christ—eternal and unchanging reality is claimed; yet something *happened*, in a given time and place, and through a given man. Here immutability and specificity are both essential to the significance and relevance of the events that are *once-for-all* (this biblical phrase concisely carries the paradox).

How resolve the paradox? If anyone could do so completely and clearly, he not only would be thinking and writing about God: he would *be* God. But here is an attempt which seeks to do justice to the universality—which the mind requires—and to the particularity—which experience makes plausible.

1. God is the One in Whom all things "live and move and have [their] being" (Acts 17:28, RSV). He is "in and under" all things; He is not out there or up there in any special way. He is *wholly other* in contradiction to a pantheism which would oversimplify and say He *is* all things; yet He is not *other* in the sense that He is *a* being apart from the various beings which have been evolved. Nothing exists apart from Him. This means that there is no reality to the category usually entitled "the supernatural." He is in and under, the Actor in all that is, i.e., *natural*.

2. As the Ultimate Ground of all, He is ultimate Power, Justice, and Love, and there is no limit to them (i.e., Him). He is uni-

formly and utterly *consistent*: His power, His judgment, His love, His self-revelation may be more manifest in one situation than in another; He is no more revelatory (though perhaps in fact more revealing) at one period in history than at another.

3. But that which by faith we attribute to Him is manifested in the particular. The vindication of His righteousness is seen in the defeat of an unfaithful and overconfident Israel by its enemies, and thus there can be taken seriously such texts as "O Assyrian, the rod of mine anger . . ." (Isa. 10:5, KJV). A particular individual can see in his own downfall, stripped of his pretenses and presumed self-sufficiency, the veritable judgment of God. The loving redemptiveness of God toward His people is seen as manifested in such datable events as the deliverance through the Red Sea, the return of the exiles from Babylon, the turning back of barbarians at the gates of Rome, the destruction by storm of the Spanish Armada (at least Anglicans would so see it, if not all Roman Catholics!) and, for particular individuals at a particular time, new hope out of despair, new security out of the death of little securities, healing of mind or body through renewal of the spirit with prayer and sacrament. And, more than all this, in the Great Particular, the going down to the grave and rising to life again of a first-century rabbi, we see operating the power, justice, and love of the eternal God.

4. Yet in no one of these particular actions or revelations— not even in *the* Action and Revelation in Jesus Christ—did God change or decide or add to or subtract from His consistent character. At *no* point, from His side of reality, did He do or say anything new, as from our side of the veil one or many of us received or perceived, or were agents of, the *new* in given situations or in the Great Situation. Opportunities for the lesser or greater entry of Judgment or Grace (as acceptance or as power) vary with the situation in personal or corporate history; but God's Judgment and Grace are constant. The occasion and resulting action or revelation is historically conditioned; the Actor-Revealer is unconditioned.

Examples may relieve the abstractness of the above; but they will necessarily be inadequate to portray the relationship of the Unconditioned to the conditioned circumstances because the examples themselves are so conditioned.

1. Why a given volcanic eruption? Primitive peoples sometimes thought that a god (an evil one harassing, or a good one duly punishing) had selected a target and sent forth the fiery lava. We believe nothing like that. The natural physical forces under the shell of the earth are already there—under pressure and ready to go. Whatever other natural factors are operative, the condition of the surface of the earth at the place of the eruption can determine the fact of an actual outpouring. If a given spot becomes thin enough, soft enough, weak enough, that which underneath functions uniformly nevertheless manifests itself in a particular event (which, if it happens within human history, becomes regarded as an historic event); something *happens* in a particular time and place.

2. A given corpus of oil does not decide to surface as a favor to an already opulent Texas millionaire. The oil is *there;* the oilman drills down to it and there is a strike.

3. A particular room is chilly in an otherwise warm, steam-heated hotel. The steam is available everywhere in the building and functions reliably; it just happens that the valve is turned off on the radiator in the given room. When the knob is turned, something *happens:* the room begins to warm. But before, during, and after, the steam was acting with constancy. The heating system did not change; the situation in the room did.

It can reasonably be objected that these examples are worse than anthropomorphism; they are the "reification" of a God who is at least personal. Granted; but in the impersonal we gain a clearer analogue for uniformity and reliability than in the personal, because the factor of human freedom introduces the quixotic or at least an existential particularity into examples drawn from human action and response. In any case the material examples serve to suggest that the paradox of uniformity and speciality can be bridged.

But is this at the expense of reducing our concept of God to that of a Great Force? Certainly He is more than that, since even man is more than that: he can, with ever-increasing skill, control, subdue, and use forces. Are we to say, for example, that the prayer of a brokenhearted lover which brings solace and new hope is simply an aperture into which can ooze something from an impersonal Strength? Most certainly not. God is not impersonal, He is not less than personal. But He is not *a* person; and hence the only safe way, by analogy, to portray the more-than-personal in Him is to move by imagination from the best "personal" as we know it, beyond. Let us turn to the image Jesus most often used.

Assume a *perfect* father. What will be his ongoing relationship to his children? Assume further that he is unlimited in his capacity to meet their needs (power), absolutely impartial in his relationship to them (justice), complete in his devotion to each and his well-being (love), and fully eager to relate to each (revelatory quality). And assume that throughout the years he or his attitude does not change in any of these regards. Still the actual relationships with his children, and with any one of them at different times, will vary—they will depend upon what now with this one, and what then with that one, calls for judgment; what opportunity there is with a particular child at a particular time to manifest love—or what capacity there is to receive it; what given needs arise to be met with what resources; what openness there is at the different stages of development in each child to appreciate the father's personality or uniqueness, or comprehend what he is like.

Now, even in this example, the father would be less than personal if he were simply passive—just waiting to be called upon for what he can bring to any given situation. In every contact in the dynamics of family life he has been open from his direction; it is simply that there have been varying degrees of openness and closedness at various times on the part of his children—and he has not imposed his will. Nor has he talked *at* them.

Now this analogy is imperfect, too, since it is impossible to erase from our minds the finitude in even a virtually perfect father that would require positive individual decisions and actions in order for his general constancy to operate. But even in the human (or "superman") picture there is suggested the correlation between unchanging reality and variable and specific involvements.

Let us now examine how this thesis works out in reference to the three convictions about experience which, as we have indicated, would appear to be most threatened by the assertion of the absolutely unconditioned character of the Ultimate Ground.

JUDGMENT AND PROVIDENCE

If a people are blinded by their own conceits, unwarrantedly sure of their security, inattentive to wrongs and weaknesses in their corporate life, and if, as a result, they fall at the hands of those they had minimized, then this indeed is the judgment of God; and those with eyes for the unseen, those who by faith know that in and under "the changes and chances of this mortal life," in and under all human strength and weakness, is consistent Power and Justice, will attribute the outcome to its Source. They probably will state this attribution in baldly anthropomorphic terms: He became more and more impatient with the nation and then decided to strike it down. It is in this form of statement that their error lies—not in the reference of all things finally to Him. It is His world; all power and righteousness are grounded in Him; He *is* Action; He is the Ultimate Cause of all. The situation brought about by the people or their leadership was the *occasion* but not the cause of the outcome.

In discussing the racial conflict in this country, a pastoral letter issued by the Episcopal Bishops in 1958, after pointing out that our nation and the Christian mission have lost much good will in the world because of our blatant discriminations, went on to say,

If America continues to lose friends as others become convinced that we do not mean what we say about justice and equality, the reason will be obvious. The judgments of the Lord are true and righteous altogether. These judgments are the plain cost we pay in God's universe for not practicing what we preach, and for not being ready to grant to others the opportunity and equality we cherish for ourselves.

In connection with this prophetic assertion, the following was said about the judgment of God:

It is not some extraneous power falling upon us with no relationship to our behavior. It is not the capricious will of an arbitrary tyrant. It is not the opinion of bishops. It is not a quotation from the Bible. God's judgment is . . . the inevitable result we bring upon ourselves when we move against the grain of His universe. It is the inevitable result of our inner contradictions. It is God frustrating our purposes when we oppose His will. . . . You will find the judgments of God reported in your daily newspaper, in the clash and contradiction of rival ambitions and fears, in the hatred and suspicion we earn when we fail to deal justly with those with whom we share this narrow world.[1]

Thus God's judgment is a *fact*—effective consistently—whether or not the one or ones judged recognize the Judge or His judgment.

Likewise with Providence. As our Lord pointed out, the rain benefits both the godly and the ungodly; the difference is that the godly—correctly—acknowledge the Source of this good; it is not this acknowledgment that makes it rain. If it were, the rain would be more evenly distributed as among the various areas where the religious reside. And to take the central image of Judaism: it would not seem that God rearranged the winds and currents at the north end of the Red Sea first to allow the crossing of the Israelites and then to drown the Egyptians in pursuit. But He was in and under the courage and wisdom of Moses and his people and the Power behind the forces of wind and wave. And Judaism became possible because those redeemed saw in all this not just a "lucky break" but the unalterable Purpose and Love of God. Thus they could sing:

I will sing to the Lord, for he has triumphed gloriously;
the horse and his rider he has thrown into the sea . . .
and he has become my salvation.

[1] Journal of the 1958 General Convention of the Episcopal Church, pp. 49-50.

Thou hast led in thy steadfast love the people whom thou
 hast redeemed,
thou has guided them by thy strength to thy holy abode.
(Exodus 15:1-2, 13, RSV)

PRAYER AND SACRAMENT

God is no "respecter of persons," and His good will toward all
men is impartial. But the degree to which His grace enters a
given life varies with the disposition of the person for it. Prayer
is a principal means for opening oneself to the power and love of
God that is already *there*—in the depths of reality. He is always
ready to guide, to inspire, to comfort, to accept, to heal, to enrich;
such barriers as there are to His thus operating in us, with us, and
through us are in each of us and in our respective situations—not
in Him. An image in the book of Revelation is suggestive here:
"Behold, I stand at the door and knock: if any man hear my
voice, and open the door, I will come in . . ." (3:20, KJV).

The various types of prayer dispose us for His "coming in." In
adoration we become more conscious of His presence (there,
whether we are conscious of it or not). In *thanksgiving* we make
evident to ourselves that He is the Ground of all that sustains
and redeems us. In *petition* we sort out our intentions and priorities
in the light of our best discernment of His purposes for us. In
intercession we broaden the basis of our concerns and sympathies
and also help to release His Power and Grace into the lives of
others (what the machinery for this is we do not know; para-
psychology or the group unconscious could be involved; but in any
case the same God to whom we are thus relating is in the depths
of the persons for whom we are praying). In *penitence* we are
seeking to understand and have removed those barriers to Him
which our own sins have erected. Therefore, though God is not
less with the man who does not pray generally, He is more
evidently with the man who does—and He is more operative in
the latter's life because the latter is more in gear with the
Ultimate Reality and hence with his own reality. A naïve, but

perhaps clarifying, example is provided by a characteristic feature of my see city: the cable car. The cable, with a fairly high degree of consistency, is always running under the open middle track. Why are some cars stopped and some running? In the case of the latter the gripman has let the clutch down to connect with the moving (note: *moving*) chain; in the case of the former, the gripman has not.

As to sacraments, in the Eucharist, for example, we speak of the Real Presence in the action or elements. And rightly; but the problem is when and where is there "the real absence"? If God is truly and fully in and under all things at all times, He is not *more* present at the Holy Communion. But in this action of remembering Christ's death and Resurrection we re-enter this continuing grace (as acceptance and power) and allow God through it to manifest the new life in us which at all times He is ready for us to have in its fullness. Thus His ever unfailing dynamic Presence is made real existentially for us at the specific time and place.

JESUS CHRIST

Now we come to the crucial problem—and glory—as to the relationship of the Unconditioned to historical events. This great Nexus we will consider in a separate chapter.

VIII: WHAT THINK
YE OF CHRIST?

O N THE capacity to answer this question depends the whole validity of what has been said before and will be said hereafter. Obviously, in all that is said He is the Center. He is the Focus of the Mighty Acts which have been presented as the heart of the Christian Faith. But if we regard God as the Ultimate Ground of Being and therefore as universal and unchanging, and if we regard the response to particular prayer, and action in particular moments of history, as simply the letting loose of the universally available Response, how can we attribute to this *particular* Person in history a final status?

Let us remind ourselves of how particular a person Jesus Christ is. It is important that we do because Christians throughout the centuries have more readily overlooked the fact that He was a true man than they have denied His divinity. Unitarianism has not been the main problem. Most of the heresies of the early Church tended in the direction of a Jesus = God approach (see App. B), and in modern times the religion of many could well be categorized as "Jesusism." But the New Testament is clear enough. Indeed, the facts have always been clear enough for any man to behold. Jesus was born in a particular place at a particular time. His mother and brothers did not understand that He had more than a human role to perform. When a ruler addressed Him as

"Good Master," He contradicted the adjective with the telling words, "Why callest thou me good? none is good, save one, that is, God" (Luke 18:19, KJV). And the early Church expressed His mind in these words: "My Father is greater than I" (John 14:28, KJV), and, "greater works" than His shall his followers do (John 14:12). He prayed to the Father.

Jesus' world-view was that of His time. The concept of the Kingdom of God which He stressed was that introduced into Judaism in the fifth century B.C., under Zoroastrian influence. He was influenced by the teaching of the Essenes, as is growing more and more evident with the availability of translations of the Dead Sea Scrolls. He had a limited mind—as is true of every man. For example, like his fellow rabbis He thought that David wrote all the Psalms and hence He quotes as of Davidic authorship Psalm 110 (which in fact is of later date) in an argument with the Pharisees. And He thought, in accord with the apocalyptic temper of his day, that the end of the world was near. All this adds up to affirm the Church's perennial teaching that He was truly man. Not Man in general: *a* man.

But the Church has always seen in Him more than a man. In Him "the Word was made flesh" (John 1:14, KJV). "God was in Christ, reconciling the world to himself" (II Cor. 5:19, RSV), "for in him dwelleth all the fulness of the Godhead bodily" (Col. 2:9, KJV). In Him there is a finality, to deny which would be to lose the whole thrust of the Christian Faith, to remove the centrality of the mighty acts of hitting bottom and' rising again. Yet to attribute finality to these mighty acts would seem to confine the fullness of the revelation and action of God to a particular moment in history in a particular place on a particular planet—thus contradicting God's universality and nonparticularity. Hence the urgency of the question, *What think ye of Christ?*

What is shown in Jesus Christ and acted out in Jesus Christ is God at his *most* natural. It is natural for Him to be revealed; here He is most revealed. That which *God is* is here most affirmed and here the total claim on human life—what *man is meant to be*

—is most affirmed. Not only did Christ teach the fullness of the law: He *was* this fullness. He lived out completely the totality of the law in the service of the Father. Nothing daunted Him; He gave to the utmost. He faced and stood up to all that would narrow the full breadth of the total claim. Nowhere on earth had this been seen before. Nor has it been known or seen since. Judged by any empirical standard, this was the perfect avenue for God to be Himself revealing and acting. In this revealing and acting we see perfect justice (the total claim), perfect love ("Father, forgive them. . ."; "This day thou shalt be with me in Paradise"), and perfect power (a continual redemption age after age of those who would accept this justice and this love and seek to make it their own). The Agent of this Reality did not *achieve* it; He so emptied Himself of self-centeredness that He could be its perfect vehicle: "He did not think to snatch at equality with God, but made himself nothing, assuming the nature of a slave. Bearing the human likeness, revealed in human shape, he humbled himself, and in obedience accepted even death—death upon a cross" (Phil. 2:6b-8, NEB). Here is the perfect avenue for God's power and revelation.

Whenever since we have observed examples of the revelation of God and of human goodness the most we can say is that this revelation is something *like* that which we have found in Jesus Christ. At no point do we ever say that Jesus Christ is like one of these others. The continued revelation of God's justice, power, and love marks the pages of Jewish history—indeed of all history —and the pages of the daily newspapers (for example, in this country and in South Africa in terms of courage in the face of racial hate). In all these intervening centuries no one has shown himself quite like Him. Were one so to show himself he would definitely be a second, and therefore not unique.

Yet, while Jesus Christ is "for us men and for our salvation" the Word made flesh, there is no reason for us to assume that— given the right historical context and given the right man responding aright—there could not be another such Incarnation. Given the right opportunity, God, who is fully present *in*, *under*, and *with* all at all times, could thus break through and be manifested in human life. In the categories of John (though they are not necessary categories),[1] the Word, the Christ, is fully in Jesus Christ, but Jesus was not the whole of the Christ: the Word went right on lighting "every man that cometh into the world" (John 1:9) even during the particular years He was incarnate in the particular man Jesus in the particular nation Israel.

Were there not the possibility of further incarnations, the Incarnation we know in Jesus Christ would be increasingly implausible as growing knowledge of the expanding universe continually reduces our sense of the uniqueness and relative importance of this particular planet. We have every reason to assume that around many of the innumerable stars, of which our sun is by no means in the largest category, are many planets; and the law of averages would suggest that there would be on any number of such earths conditions which support life and that on many of these the evolutionary and historical process has progressed to the point that some beings thereon are capable of relationship with God. If the Christian Faith required us to believe that only on *this* one little planet, this one instance of the hundreds, thousands—maybe millions—of possibilities, God was enabled to break through in terms of a genuine human life, then belief in our Incarnation here would be difficult indeed. All too obvious would be the geocentric parochialism in such a view—understandably accepted before Copernicus, rationally impossible since.

Yet on this very planet, whole continents went for millennia without knowledge of the Christ. It might well be asked, Why did not God become fully incarnate in other places and times on *this* earth?

In answer we can affirm two things:

1. The fact is He hasn't, to our knowledge. And no other religion claims that He has.

2. On the other hand, God has "left not himself without

---

[1] See Chap. X as to this and also as to the creedal affirmation concerning Christ as "only begotten . . . before all worlds."

witness" anywhere or anytime (Acts 14:17, KJV). The same Word revealed in Jesus Christ is revealed "at sundry times and in divers manners" (Heb. 1:1, KJV), not only through the prophets but through seekers after truth, beauty and meaning in all cultures and eras. The breadth of the revelation of God has been beautifully portrayed in Dr. Percy Dearmer's hymn:

> Sing praise to God, who spoke through man
> In differing times and manners,
> For those great seers who've led the van,
> Truth writ upon their banners;
> For those who once blazed out the way,
> For those who still lead on to-day,
> To God be thanks and glory.
>
> For Amos, of the prophets first
> The vast confusion rending
> Of many gods that blest or curst,
> To find One, good, transcending;
> For all who taught mankind to rise
> Out of the old familiar lies,
> To God be thanks and glory.
>
> For Socrates who, phrase by phrase,
> Talked men to truth, unshrinking,
> And left for Plato's mighty grace
> To mold our ways of thinking;
> For all who wrestled, sane and free,
> To win the unseen reality,
> To God be thanks and glory.
>
> For all the poets who have wrought
> Through music, words, and vision
> To tell the beauty of God's thought
> By art's sublime precision,
> Who bring our highest dreams to shape
> And help the soul in her escape,
> To God be thanks and glory.[1]

So in the revelation in Jesus Christ the uniqueness lies not in the *fact* of revelation or in the Source of what is revealed, but rather

[1] The [Episcopal] Hymnal 1940, Hymn 299.

in the Avenue of that Source's revelation—at the right time the right man related aright to Him who is ever there and ready to be revealed. He was totally open to the Source, the Ultimate Ground of all that is.

His divinity is in the fullness of His true humanity, His total readiness to be a man, that is, the full, active vehicle of God's meaning and love. But this possibility is in all men. This is why the passage quoted above on Jesus' servanthood and obedience opens with the words: "Let this mind be in you, which was also in Christ Jesus . . ." (Phil. 2:5, KJV). Some men had in a measure shown this capacity before; some have shown it since. It is ever a possibility. But this possibility—in its fullness—would not have been an actuality until the *kairos*—the right time, the time when men were ready for God thus to be revealed, the time into which One could be born who would be ready. Israel in that century was the right time and place, and Jesus was ready. The one Source of all was recognized; the claim had already been recognized: and He, with the authority of the Source, pushed the claim to the absolute limit. He did not deny the value of accepted rules in stating certain duties within the claim; but He honestly declared that the codified law of His day was inadequate to encompass the claim; indeed, He saw in the assertions of particular elements of the law the minimization of the over-all obligation. In asserting its totality He in effect ordered His own death. It has been impossible safely so to disturb the mores in any time, and He carried this disturbance to the limit. Built into Jesus' assertion of the whole claim of God was the Cross. And in this Cross the redemptiveness of God inevitably appeared in action. Likewise, built into this assertion of the claim (justice) and the demonstration of forgiveness (love), *God being fully in this,* was vindication through the Resurrection (power), i.e., eternal life. God was in and under (as He is always in and under all things) all this. His power to vindicate is as strong as His power to reveal and to love.

Hence, Christians are those who see in this man in history, this particular man in a particular time and place, the all-out acting out of the being of God, Who is the whole Ground of all being, Who was always like this and always will be like this.

Thus as to the "scandal of particularity," there is nothing particular about all this as far as some special decision on God's part is concerned: He did not decide to be that way just then. But there is particularity in this manifestation. No manifestation, no letting loose of that which is already there would have any relation to human life and destiny unless it were in a particular time and place. When, as a bishop, I say that one of our priests is a good pastor, I am referring only, when it comes right down to it, to my knowledge of good pastoral care in particular situations. I cannot make a generalization—not one that would be of any value—apart from these particulars. The priest was particularly helpful to a particular mother when a particular daughter died under particular circumstances at a particular time, and so forth. Similarly God could not thus be released really to be known to man except at a particular time and place. And that is the way it was— and hence is. Here God was not being quixotic, special, miraculous, or supernatural, but was being Himself—*natural*. Through the free choice of Jesus Christ (and if He was not free He was not a man) God could be truly Himself with men. This many have known, and do know, by faith (there is no other way). But we cannot, through our experience on this small planet revolving around a secondary star, say that such a full revelation could not be known otherwise on another of the many, many, many planets on which there might be perceptive life (capable of receiving revelation), or could not be known otherwise on this planet. From the limited perspective of a short-term civilization on this particular aggregation of matter we could not make such an assertion without virtually deifying ourselves. But here on this planet among the men we know and with whom we are in fellowship historically and presently, *this* Truth has been made manifest. And in and through this we know, as much as we can know, what God expects our life to be like, and what He is like toward us. Thus we can assert honestly, in the words of the Nicene Creed, that Jesus Christ is "God of God, Light of Light, Very God of Very God." He is the One against whom we would measure any other reported experience—through all the centuries ahead, as to any other human life, or as to any life on any planet. This is enough for us, and we know that God so revealed would be enough for anyone anywhere in any world.

IX: HIS DEATH
AND RESURRECTION

THE FOREGOING pages simply *assume* that the death of Jesus has a point beyond mere miscarriage of justice, and that the Resurrection of Jesus is a fact. A Christian does make these assumptions —and must—to *be* a Christian. But on what basis?

First, the Cross.

Practically no one any more doubts that the crucifixion happened. What it meant historically is plain enough. As the freshest (in both senses of the word) rabbi of His day, Jesus ended up exposed on too many fronts at once.

He had concluded that His time was short; the preaching of the present power of the Kingdom and the opening of men to its reality He put first. So he did not throw himself into the revolutionary nationalist movement of his day, and hence He put off the Zealots—losing Judas and his like.[1]

He was with the Pharisees in their religious seriousness (unique then or in any era) and their conviction about eternal life; but he did not subscribe to their ethically suffocating legalism. (He was most "with" them; hence He was harshest toward them.)

In almost every word He uttered He stood against the Saduccees. They were the power-structure of Israel at that time. In relation

[1] The relative (cf. I and II Macc.) unfruitfulness of this cause was proved in A.D. 70 when the revolt of the Jews brought an end (until the establishment of the State of Israel in 1948) to the nation.

to the Roman overlordship, they were the Quislings, the collabora-tionists. And they had control of the biggest local industry, the Temple, with its concessions: the sale of animals (doves and others) for sacrifice, and the changing of money. He felt that their profitable emphasis on the externals of religion was a princi-pal block to the real thing. His reticence as to the Zealots and His quarrels (in which He came out very well) with the Pharisees were one thing; but His dramatic action against the Saduccees (the Establishment) interfered with "business as usual." He in-volved himself in a "demonstration": He went right into the Court of the Gentiles of the Temple and let all the animals (in-cluding birds) out of their cages and knocked over the carefully arranged tables of the bankers. That did it.

A fourth front is important. The Government got into it. The cynical Roman colonialists couldn't have cared less about indige-nous theological quarrels. Pilate and his colleagues, assigned to Israel, had no constructive program for the development of the area and were simply holding on—and didn't want the boat rocked. That might interfere with a nice next assignment.

So, from every point of view, Jesus had to go. And He did.

At His trial (the jurisdictional questions are complicated: law-yers, including the author, have been puzzled ever since), He pleaded *nolo contendere*. Which, in effect, means: I am here, my record is obvious: What then?

The answer (reluctantly given) was capital punishment.

Now this very best example of such all-out courage (because He took on everybody, really—the power-structure, the Govern-ment, the radicals, the pious) is inspiring, especially to those who try (not always successfully) to be out on no more than one front at a time. But is it ultimately *the* thing?

Yes, it is. The martyrs, the prophets of the old and the new Israel, some of the clergy and the laity (we hope with Christian, not just secular, inspiration) have shown great courage in moments of crisis (the civil rights struggle of our own day affords many examples). But none of these have had such an assorted collection of enemies (not only of Him, but of the Truth), and none have exposed themselves on *all* fronts. Further, not one of them has so fully as Jesus been open at all points to God's full manifestation. But He was; so this was—and is—the Great Moment, the Great Break-through. For everything that has happened, before or since, God made it—*fully.*

Here *He* displays the sickness, here *He* provides the Cure. We are met in this. And in everything. The glorious affiliation of the Ultimate Good with total weakness and total hope is shown—and done. That is enough.

Some of the Church's other expressed views are nonsense. Item: God had to have a body sacrificed to Him—to pay Him off. What kind of God! (What kind of a man, even?) As to such a God, atheism is admirable. Item: Someone had to fight—and win—against the Devil. Maybe—but where is this Devil?—and if there be such, he is still doing very well, as anyone reading the daily papers can know.

Enough that *total weakness* and *maximum hope* is displayed. That is as much ultimately as most of us will grasp. Here is displayed the Atonement. A most illuminating word, this; not as a pun, but etymologically, it means *at-one-ment.* In it, torn man can be put back together again.

Did the hope prevail in the end? Yes. Personal ongoingness is a fact—for everybody. The person is more than the body. The person shapes the body—in many ways—including its size (if he is wise). Men have, in all cultures, yearned for going on after death. For every other basic yearning there has been some reality corresponding to it. Hunger: there is such a thing as food—unavailable as we make it for so many in our world. Sex: there is such a thing as sexual fulfillment—unavailable as it is for some, owing to circumstances, physical or psychological barriers, or the mores. Clothing against the cold: there is such, though many lack it by reason of others' indifference. The yearning for ongoing personal life: it is not too much to assume that for this yearning too there is a matching reality.

But for Christians eternal life is not merely an assumption. Jesus had affirmed it unqualifiedly; and the actual experience of the risen Christ's presence among them convinced His disciples of the truth of His affirmation. The utterly convincing quality of His appearances (as compared with other apparitions—actual or reported) is not surprising, considering His total openness to the Ground of all reality.[2] What had been (and today, without this belief, is) philosophical speculation, now is experienced as reality— and is God's gift. And through those who first knew, many others through the centuries have shared this confidence—both as to themselves and as to the rest of the Communion of Saints.

This belief is not simply a bargaining on futures. The believer can experience a here-and-now involvement in eternal life. The time you are spending reading this book is as much a part of eternal life as any comparable period beyond death. Those who express diffidence about the afterlife in such a phrase as "one world at a time" are stating a half-truth, a good half-truth. It is *now* we are to live—and experience and act upon the fullness of God's gift of eternal life. But we can do so with more courage knowing that these days are not all there is. We are involved in a very long-range program.

[2] Christians are free to hold different views as to the precise mode of the Resurrection; in fact, the biblical accounts themselves differ—e.g., it takes a different type of body to eat a fish (John 21:13) than to walk through a closed door (John 20:26). The most satisfactory image is that of the "psychical body" elaborated upon in I Cor. 15:20-58. In the latter passage St. Paul is encompassing resurrection in general as well as Christ's Resurrection.

X: THE TRINITY

THE JEWS who became Christians came into the movement with an uncomplicated monotheism. God was conceived of in personal terms—as one person. The Gentile converts were of two orientations: The more sophisticated minority, influenced by Greek philosophy, were monotheistic, but their conception of God was less personal than that of the Jews, and hence, all the more, not multipersonal. The majority of the Gentiles had been polytheistic, believing in several divine persons, but they had not characteristically grouped these persons under the conception of a single being.

How then did the doctrine of the Trinity arise?

In late Old Testament writings and in the Apocrypha a new image began to appear: the Spirit of God or Wisdom. In continuity with this trend Jesus speaks of the Spirit, the Holy Spirit; and the New Testament writers do also, sometimes phrasing it as the Spirit of Christ. The precise meaning of this category is not clear; nor did its use require any writer to develop a new theory about God's nature and make-up.

The same is true of the response of the early Christians to Jesus—as ultimate. It was possible for the apostles, evangelists, and teachers to proclaim the mighty acts of God in Christ without any reconstruction of the doctrine of God—and this during the period of the Church's most rapid growth.

But as the Church became more and more Gentile in its membership, and as its prevailing mode of thought changed from action or *verb*–thinking to analytical or *noun*–thinking (see p. 35), it was felt important to get down in black and white the nature and relationship of three experiences of the Ultimate: the Father, the Christ, and the Spirit. This is a natural enough development: one is called to worship with his whole mind as well as his whole heart; and accordingly, as J. V. Langmead Casserly has pointed out, if a philosopher becomes a Christian he must become a Christian philosopher.[1] But some of the early attempts at putting the picture together threatened to produce distortions of the truth experienced. One theory compromised monotheism, another the ultimacy of Christ, another the ultimacy of the Spirit; still another the consistently ongoing reality of that which is experienced in Christ and in the Spirit.

And, just as in the case of the process of the crystallization of Christology, official pronouncements meant as fences against heresy became the normative definitions of divine reality. As would be expected, these attempts to state relationships were packaged in the going concepts and words of the day, ones developed in Greek philosophy. By this time the Western Church was sufficiently important that the capacity of the Latin language to provide carriers for the definitions was involved, as well as the availability of adequate Greek words. And matching up the two sets of words became a problem.

The words which came into the picture were these:

GREEK	LATIN	MEANING
1. *ousia*	*essentia*	being
2. *hypostasis*	*substantia*	that which underlies phenomena, actually a synonym for 1.
3. *prosopon*	*persona*	a particular manifestation of one or many realities; e.g., a mask used when a single actor was playing several parts in a play, or actor-in-mask.

In an attempt to underline the monotheism some had used *prosopon* for Father, Christ, and Spirit (Sabellianism; see App.

---

[1] *The Christian in Philosophy* (New York: Scribner's, 1955), p. 11.

C); but the orthodox decided that this destroyed the ongoing reality of the Three. Hence there was drafted into service a possible narrower meaning of *hypostasis*, that which underlies particular reality (in contrast to reality in general); and the answer to the problem was phrased as three *hypostases* in one *ousia*. One would think that the Latin Church, which really did not believe differently, would have kept the parallels outlined above and spoken of God as three *substantiae* in one *essentia*. But *essentia* had become an archaic word, and hence the Latins moved down one notch and for the One used *substantia*, the equivalent of what the Greeks used for Three; and for each of the Three they used *persona*, the equivalent of *prosopon*—which the Church had already discarded as implying that each one of the Three was simply an on-and-off phase of the One.

But in the end *persona* did not carry this implication. In fact, quite the contrary: the word "person" more and more—and this trend reached its height in the Renaissance—began to stand for individual, unique, autonomous personality. So instead of the danger that people would be misled by the word to believe that Father, Son, and Holy Ghost are merely masks that God is wearing at different times and in different situations, the peril has long been the reverse: the implication of tritheism—in spite of the clear intent of the Fathers to the contrary.

The practical result—the way Christianity looks (not only to the outsider, but to many an insider)—reminds one of the story about some American tourists being guided around Trinity College, Oxford, by the Dean. The session had been so long and tedious and the visitors so inquisitive that the decanal guide was becoming more and more casual. Finally, pointing to a series of carvings high up on a building, one of the tourists asked, "What are those?"

"Gargoyles," the Dean grunted.

"But what do they stand for?" the visitor pressed.

"Oh," hardly looking up, the Dean replied, "The Trinity—for Trinity College."

"But there are four of them," interposed the guest.

Then really looking up this time, the Dean retorted, "Yes, to be sure: three persons and one God."

Revealing as to the inevitable confusion is the name chosen for the religious movement dispensing with the divinity of Christ: "Unitarianism" (when all Christians are, as to the doctrine of God, supposed to be Unitarian). And likewise the commonplace definition stated in humor by orthodox Christians: "A Unitarian is one who believes, at the most, in one God." Revealing too is the explanation commonly given, even by churchmen, for the fact that Islamic evangelism is more successful in some parts of Africa than Christian missonary effort: "The natives, on leaving their polytheism, prefer a more straightforward monotheism."

As we seek to employ the Trinitarian formula today we are hobbled by at least three difficulties:

1. As we have seen, the words used were not adequate or consistent even in the period in which they were adopted.

2. Meanwhile, the word "substance," no longer a useful carrier of meaning in physics, has even less meaning in the less precise conceptuality of metaphysics.

3. Similarly, the use of the word "person" distorts, as we have seen; originally it said too little, now it says too much: originally, Father, Christ, and Spirit as mere masks of God, now, three divine personalities.

So at the worst the tritheism has been implied; at the best, confusion and a sense of irrelevance has been engendered. As to the latter, Cardinal Cushing of Boston recently provided a telling illustration in an address at a meeting of Episcopal priests. As a parish priest he was called to the side of a man who had collapsed on the floor in a department store. The then Father Cushing asked the man, "Do you believe in God the Father, God the Son, and God the Holy Ghost?" The latter opened one eye and said to those standing about, "Here I am dying, and he's asking me riddles!"

Is a conceptualized doctrine of the Trinity in fact needed in order to preserve the essentials of the Christian Faith? If the answer is No, then it is evident that the Church's mission would be relieved of a heavy piece of luggage. The traditional formulation—no matter how "explained" on the one hand, or shrouded in mystery on the other—is as a plain matter of fact a barrier to *rapprochement* with several groups. With the Jews (Martin Buber, who is quite well informed as to Christian theology, once said to me, "I know what you Christians are trying to say by the doctrine of the Trinity, but why do you have to say it that way?"), with the Muslims, and indeed with many non-Church people who at least vaguely assume a theistic universe.

Obviously, an essential of the Faith should not be abandoned or played down, even if it does make conversion to, or understanding of, Christianity more difficult. But we have good precedent for de-essentializing things heretofore held essential, when the given false absolutization markedly interferes with the mission of the Church. Under the stimulus of St. Paul, the First Council of Jerusalem (Acts 15:6-29) relieved Christianity of the obligation of Jewish ceremonial observances, e.g., circumcision and dietary restrictions —at first held to be essential by such leaders as Peter, James, and John. In the nineteenth and twentieth centuries, principal Christian Churches have one by one suffered or encouraged their scholars and spokesmen to deny, interpret as myth, or to ignore portions of the Scriptures which were proving embarrassing in the light of scientific and historical discoveries and of literary criticism of the biblical texts. Yet up to that time it was by and large regarded as essential to believe in the *ipsissima verba* of the Scriptures. Without this openness we would not in recent decades have experienced such a marked number of conversions to the Christian Faith on the part of members of the academic community— and of other educated persons as well.

The Church's classical way of stating what is represented by the doctrine of the Trinity has in fact been a barrier with the well educated and less educated alike. *And it is not essential to the Christian Faith.* These considerations support this conclusion:

1. The apostles and the other first followers of the Way never heard of it. Were they not Christians?

2. All that can be said of the Holy Spirit can be said of God without attribution to a distinct Person in the Godhead. In fact all that is said officially of the Third Person was already said of the Spirit of God, the Wisdom of God, or the Spirit of Christ, in the Old Testament, the Apocrypha, and the New Testament before the Councils declared the Trinitarian formulation. And the writers who used such phrases did not define a separate entity but were stressing a particular way of God's relationship to us, a way integral to His very being.[2]

As check points, let us use the particular affirmations about the Holy Ghost in the Nicene Creed (there are none in the Apostles' Creed):

a. The Lord: This is true of God as such.

b. The Giver of Life: From Genesis 1 on this is affirmed of God.

c. Who proceedeth from the Father (the ancient form still left this way by the Eastern Churches): this, in existential terms, affirms the thesis. If we add (on Papal authority only, eleventh century) the *filioque* (and the Son) clause, the same is true: Hence the relevance of the reference to the Spirit of Christ in the New Testament, in which there is no Trinitarian definition.

d. Who spake by the prophets: We need only recollect the familiar phrase in the prophetic books: "Thus spake the Lord God . . ."

The points above can be answered by saying, "This only proves what the Trinitarian doctrine has affirmed all along, namely, that the Holy Ghost is truly God." But rather they illustrate that it is not essential to think of the Holy Ghost as a separate Person.

3. What is affirmed as characteristic of "the Second Person" is also affirmable of God in general.

a. He is the Word: and note the careful ambiguity in John 1: "The Word was with God and the Word was God." The Word reveals ("This is the light that lighteth every man that cometh

---

[2] Hence this view is not Sabellianism or Modalism, i.e., that we simply *experience* God in those ways (See App. C).

into the world"); but God as such has always been revealing (cf. Genesis to Revelation where, far more often than not, there is no reference to the Word or Christ, and certainly none to the Second Person of the Trinity.) There are references to the Holy Spirit as revealing. And in the field of systematic theology there is an overlap concerning two topics: the General Revelation of the Word and the Secular Work of the Holy Spirit. Thus within these terms of reference we can ask: Granting that God is revealing His truth, in a measure at least, through a Buddha or a Freud, is it the Word or the Holy Spirit who is the Revealer? The Second Person or the Third Person?

b. The Second Person is said to be involved in Creation: "through whom all things were made." Yet almost everywhere in the Bible, Creation is attributed to God directly; and philosophically, we can find plausible that it is He who is the Evolver and Sustainer of all things, in whom we live and move and have our being (Acts 17:28). There is neither need for, nor plausibility in, this extra layer of operation—a remnant of the gnostoid *logos* philosophy so influential in Christian and sophisticated pagan thought of the early second century.

Then what of the doctrine of the pre-existence of Christ? What of such biblical affirmations as "in the beginning was the Word" (John 1:1), "God, who created all things by Jesus Christ" (Eph. 3:9), "[Christ is] the firstborn of every creature: For by him were all things created . . . And he is before all things, and by him all things consist" (Col. 1:15-17, KJV). And what of the creedal affirmation, "the only-begotten Son of God; begotten of his Father before all worlds"?

Obviously these affirmations do not refer to Jesus the man of Nazareth. Were the human Jesus coexistent with the Father from all eternity and His agent in creation, He would not have been a true man, one who in His youth "increased in wisdom and in stature, and in favor with God and man" (Luke 2:52, RSV), and who conceived of Himself in relation to the Father as a Son. What is referred to by these biblical and creedal affirmations is not simply Jesus of Nazareth, but the *Christ*, the Word—terms which reflect that which is eternal in God, unchangably from all eternity into all eternity. It is this ever outgoing nature and dynamic of God that creates, through the evolutionary process, and reveals—wherever, but centrally "for us men and for our salvation" in Jesus. It is that in God which men have called the Word or the Christ which creates and reveals. To affirm this does not require belief in a distinct Person serving as the Agent of the Father. Better that we affirm the Incarnation really boldly: *The Ultimate Ground is fully in it;* the same—and only—Ultimate Ground who is the Source, Evolver, Energizer, Savior, Sustainer, and Inspirer of all that is.

c. The Second Person is Redeemer. But the story of several thousand years of the People of God have shown us that *God as such* has been redemptive—long before anyone heard or conceived of the Word, the Christ, or Jesus Christ. We need only recall the saga of Noah and the Ark, the outcome of the Abraham–Isaac sacrifice myth, the Joseph saga, the mighty acts in the bondage–Exodus experience, the deliverance and restoration of the people Israel over and over, the Old Testament healing narratives[3] and prophetic assurances. What at bottom is revealed about the nature of God in the Cross that is not already said (though not uniquely and cosmically acted out by Jesus on the Cross) in the action and words passed on to us through the prophet Hosea? The Scriptures are a glorious pageant of a healing, redeeming, restoring God—always this, and ever this.

d. The Second Person, incarnated and resurrected, reigns. All that Jesus was, did, and said is permanent and eternal in reality and significance, yes. This is an important meaning of the Ascension.[4] But what does this say other than that God reigns, that His realm and those engaged in it reign with Him forever, that this God, involved as always (but uniquely in the Person of, and

---

[3] Generally overlooked by Christians, owing to our innocently Marcionite preaching and, in most Churches at present, to their virtual absence from the liturgy.

[4] And the Resurrection narratives and the account of the Transfiguration, depending upon our assessment of the word of various New Testament scholars as to which are "doublets" with which.

mighty acts through, Jesus Christ) in the life and reality of His evolved creation, has in Him (as He is totally in it) all that is, all that abides, all things that are "true and pure and lovely and of good report."[5]

e. He (the Christ, the Second Person) shall come to judge. Tenses are not very accurate in phrasing ultimate things.[6] Obviously He always judges: I am this moment judged—in this very act of writing. And there is a permanence in the formula, claim —behavior—judgment: a permanence apparently best expressible, in our finite fragmentation of time–eternity, by the future tense. But who judges? The One who always has judged: God. Not up on a throne, with Jesus sitting on the right like a Suffragan Bishop, and the Holy Ghost sitting on the left like an Archdeacon. *Just God.* The Ultimate Ground of our being at every instant is in contrast to our existential exercise of the gift of being that *is* each of us. This is the God that was in Jesus Christ fully manifesting the terms and scope of this judgment. So Christ is not left out; but there is no need to think of a distinct Person as the Judge.

What, then, of the doctrine of the Trinity?

First, we must recognize that it has been—and is—relatively valuable as an earthen vessel. If one wants to organize God, why not this way as well as any other?

For many today even, the Trinity-in-Unity apparatus seems to provide a satisfactory, and satisfying, vehicle for apprehending and expressing, as much as finite minds can, what God is and has done and ever does. But what is essential behind it is that *God is;* that He is true to His revelation of Himself; that He is in all and, when we let Him, *can* break through; that He *has* broken through —uniquely in Jesus Christ; that He does, and ever will; that He is fully with it throughout; that all that has been attributed to each of the three Persons, He just *is.* Ever was and ever will be.

One of the presuppositions of the Freudian method in psychoanalysis is that a problem can sometimes be handled if its genesis

---

[5] Book of Common Prayer, p. 596; based on Phil. 4:8.

[6] As to this problem of eschatological writing, try out the Michaelmas epistle: Rev. 12:7-12.

is understood. If categories of thought involved in the classical formulation of the Trinity are no longer viable, then we need not feel troubled by them in regard to the conventional Trinitarian declaration. This, *provided* that (*a*) we continue to affirm about God—and as integral to Him—all that heretofore has been experienced of Him, and heretofore attributed to a given Person of the Trinity; and (*b*) we use with a sense of reality the liturgical formulae of the respective Churches, not disdaining the basis of their ideological development, but respecting the serious theological enterprise which resulted in these now dated definitions. This last proviso is particularly important for those of us in Churches where the reform of liturgically fixed statements is bogged down by our very democracy: in the meantime we can attribute a genuine measure of truth to outdated concepts and semantics.

Jesus warned us against putting new wine in old bottles: The bottles might burst. They might—indeed they will. Let us put in the new wine—or the new fruit of the old and eternal Vine; and *let* them burst. Then perhaps the Churches, even through their democratic processes, may provide the new bottles. A church *can* and *has* (and henceforth let them hold their peace who say it *cannot* be done). Here, as evidence, is a new way of saying *Credo*:

We believe in God, the Eternal Spirit, Father of our Lord Jesus Christ and our Father, and to his deeds we testify:
    He calls the worlds into being
        creates man in his own image
        and sets before him the ways of life and death.
    He seeks in holy love to save all people from aimlessness
        and sin.
    He judges men and nations by his righteous will
        declared through prophets and apostles.
    In Jesus Christ, the man of Nazareth, our crucified and
        risen Lord, he has come to us
        and shared our common lot,
        conquering sin and death
        and reconciling the world to himself.
    He bestows upon us his Holy Spirit,
        creating and renewing the Church of Jesus Christ,

binding in covenant faithful people of all ages,
tongues and races.
He calls us into his Church
to accept the cost and joy of discipleship
to be his servants in the service of men,
to proclaim the gospel to all the world
and to resist the powers of evil,
to share in Christ's baptism and eat at his table,
to join him in his passion and victory.
He promises to all who trust him
forgiveness of sins and fullness of grace,
courage in the struggle for justice and peace,
his presence in trial and rejoicing,
and eternal life in his kingdom which has no end.
Blessing and honor, glory and power be unto him. Amen.[7]

[7] Statement of Faith, United Church of Christ, adopted by the Second
General Synod, 1959.

XI: AN APOLOGIA
FOR EARTHEN VESSELS

W<small>HEN THE</small> false gods have been dethroned, leaving God alone enthroned, then, as Søren Kierkegaard has reminded us, they can be reinstated—in subordination to the true God. Likewise once the nonabsolute character of the categories of Creed, Code, and Cult has been recognized, and the absolute character of the Ultimate Ground, His claim, and His mighty acts have been affirmed, then many of the "earthen vessels" can be reinstated.

We *are* called to carry the treasure. And since we are finite beings locked into time and history, able to communicate only through words and symbols, we are able to think and assess our feelings only through concepts and propositions. Although these words, symbols, and concepts are temporal and conditioned, without them we cannot think or speak or write at all. Therefore, if we are to carry the treasure we must do so in *some* set of earthen vessels.

Must these vessels be newly selected in each age? If the given definition, myth, or symbol actually does not today fit the reality as perceived (or perhaps never did) the Church should be no less conscientious than the Pure Food and Drug Administration or the Federal Trade Commission in guarding against inadequate packaging or mislabeling. On the other hand, a given earthen vessel need not be discarded just *because* it is old, or another one drafted into service just *because* it is new. In truth, as we shall see, if the vessel passes the test of adequacy, the fact of antiquity is a plus (though not a determinative one), just as, for other reasons, the fact of novelty can be an aid to communication.

The primary test is adequacy—not in some abstract sense, but *adequacy of communication in a given culture in a given period of its history.* Thus in the task of theological reconstruction (a task appropriate in any period and always undertaken belatedly), we should expect several different dispositions of orthodox propositions, rules, symbols, and myths, or what some regard as myths:

1. Abolition (or quiet shelving *sub silentio*).
2. Salvaging: a reform or "cleaning up" of the picture, retaining its principal elements.
3. Preservation intact with interpretation "loud and clear."

In short, there is no generic answer to what to do with "the teaching of the Church," its "unchanging moral law," its machinery, its choreography. The answers should be—and are being—arrived at eclectically. Not quixotically, but in terms of the norm spelled out above: *adequacy.*

What elements of "purity of heart" should be to the fore for those who care enough about the victory of the gospel to engage here? Certainly at least these: *candor*—let's not say what we don't really mean; *modesty*—what we select afresh will be as tentative and historically conditioned as almost anything that has been rejected; and *courage*—a lot of people won't like it and will shout epithets at us.

Whatever we come up with, most people (both the faithful and seekers) do want to feel that what we are setting forth has more authentication than the word of the spokesman. And they should. It is a given we are to preach and teach and witness to, a Reality that precedes and on which *we* depend. There is a pervasive and appropriate yearning for *continuity*; indeed, in the group-unconscious, there is a nostalgia for abiding archetypes and even words. Forms that respond to this yearning are supports to stability not only of the culture generally and of the institutional Church, but also of the individual in his integration.

The external that provides this advantage is rarely, if ever, "from the beginning"; but it may serve the purpose if it is continuous enough to embrace the lifetime of the person thus aided, or better still if it is old enough for its origins to be lost in the mists of history (at least as far as the given individual's knowledge is concerned: not many of our laymen—and not all of our clergy— are well acquainted with the history of doctrine, liturgy, or moral theology). There is a real relevance here to the injunction, "Thou shalt not remove thy neighbor's landmark" (Deut. 19:14, KJV). We must take it away if it wrongly marks the land, but if it is more or less accurate in location we should certainly leave it be.

Further, part of the value in worship, preaching, and ceremonial is communication to, and nourishing of, the unconscious mind. The capacity of ideas to reach this level depends on well-worn paths into the unconscious level; hence the importance of continuity of symbols and phrases.[1]

But there is one danger in the old words, the old ways. People can become numb to them—cease to "hear," cease to perceive. Thus it is not surprising that a reading from a modern translation of the Scriptures—for example, from The New English Bible, or from J. B. Phillips' or Monsignor Knox's translations (in the case of the latter two, "paraphrases" is perhaps a more apt word)— can have an electrifying effect on a congregation; some may not like it, but nearly all listen. So too with the restoration of meaningful ancient ceremonies which better involve the congregation and vividly proclaim the meaning and hence do not require esoteric knowledge or wordy explanation.[2]

In preaching, a restatement of the doctrine of Justification in terms of the psychological problem of the reconciliation of self-

[1] See, more fully, my Beyond Anxiety, Chap. IX.

[2] E.g., as part of the Liturgical Movement as expressed in more and more Roman Catholic and Anglican Churches today, the Gospel Procession, the Offertory Procession, and the Pax (greeting). See App. D.

criticism and self-acceptance—if true to the basic dynamics of judgment and grace—can "speak" to men's condition, as the old words cannot—or at least generally do not.

So the old affirms continuity and the new brings relevance. How assert *relevant continuity*? What do we keep, what do we modify, what do we discard?

There is no final answer. If there were, it would represent the restoration of a series of absolutes less than the Absolute, the denial of all that has been said before. The specifics of any answer must represent, at most, the best that can be provided by those of our time and place for our time and place. I do not claim that these pages represent that best; and in any case, since once below the level of the Absolute we are dealing with relativities, every thoughtful reader will have his own particular set of answers to the question of achieving relevant continuity. The following summary is offered only as a considered sample of a way to hold the treasure —in vessels—without (hopefully) losing, obscuring, or adulterating the treasure.

1. *Abolition.* The most important thing is to eliminate all spatial images, not only about God but about all of unseen Reality. Away with all that suggests *limited scope* for the Divine—one thing among other things, one domain aside other domains. Away with all gestures, verbal distinctions, tones of voice that suggest a separation of the sacred and the secular, of God and His world, of spiritual and material—no reverent pointing up at the words "our Heavenly Father," no pious looking up to heaven. Let our gestures (and there are appropriate ones) suggest the here-ness and now-ness of the Ultimate Ground; let our words suggest (they can never describe) the aliveness of all that is, with His presence, His availability, His ever-readiness to break through; the intended (and realizable) goodness of all people and things through Him; the holiness of all moments, all confrontations. Let our words and symbols allow Him *in*, not relegate Him to a corner—however holy that corner is pictured as being.

As for words, we should replace as soon as possible all terms which have little or no meaning for modern ears (even for people with a reasonable amount of education), such as "vouchsafe," "prevent" (a combination of "go before" and "direct"), "propitiation," "succour."

As for readings, since the very fact of a lectionary for the Church year presupposes a process of selection from a larger body of material, i.e., the whole Bible, we should not include among our choices passages of Scripture which present a view of God and His attitudes and actions in contradiction to the kind of God we actually believe in. For example: It is understandable, in the light of the history of many tribal and national groups in various eras, that the Israelites took over land belonging to other tribes. Early English colonizers of this country did the same to the Indians; Americans did the same to the Mexicans in Texas and California. But just as in the case of the latter two illustrations (and in the case of the many movements of peoples to various parts of Europe and Asia), we do not believe that God ordained these conquests, few of us would believe that God, with love for all men—including the Israelites—would justify the deliberate attempt to destroy—or make refugees of—the Canaanites and other residents of the Eastern end of the Mediterranean, in order that the Hebrews might have it their way. We do not solemnly read in Church (even in my diocese) historical passages about the way Americans, infiltrating California, arranged to form an independent nation (the California Republic) by way of a revolution in order that this fair land might be grafted into the United States of America; so there is no reason why we should read unto God's glory of the exploits of the Israelites in their quite understandable expansionism—this material not even being susceptible to mythological interpretation in order to express a legitimate meaning.

The same basis of critique is applicable to many other biblical passages where the lector and the hearers (if they reflect) know that we by no means could stand by what is being read. Nor in the singing or reading of the Psalms should we include verses which,

due either to a faulty Hebrew text that makes adequate translation impossible or to the wrong-headedness of the ideas expressed,
present views of God or man that we would not be prepared to
affirm as true or good. Incidentally, this process has already begun
in a small measure; e.g., in the Book of Common Prayer, the
setting apart by a space of Psalm 69:23-36 and Psalm 137:7-9
(even to the most insensitive it seemed shocking to follow "Blessed
shall he be that taketh thy children and throweth them against
the stones" with "Glory be to the Father, . . ."), and the
elimination in a number of portions of the Anglican Communion
of the rather harsh verses 8-11 of the original *Venite* (Ps. 95).

As for prayers, we should not put into the mouths of clergy
words which in no wise correspond to our teaching about God:
for example, the first Collect appointed in the Episcopal Office of
the Communion of the Sick, with its phrase "who dost correct
those whom thou dost love, and chastise everyone whom thou dost
receive," (and its accompanying selection for the Epistle: "My son,
despise not thou the chastening of the Lord; do not faint when
thou art rebuked of him: for whom the Lord loveth he chasteneth,
and scourgeth every son whom he receiveth"). These are in direct
contradiction to our Lord's teaching that sickness is not necessarily
to be attributed to God's punishment for sin. Nor should we
perpetuate such fanciful medieval speculations as that reflected in
the Prayer of Humble Access in the Anglican Eucharist: "so to eat
the flesh of thy dear son Jesus Christ and to drink His blood, that
our sinful *bodies* may be made clean by His *body*, and our *souls*
washed through His most precious *blood*"; or such utterly meaningless references as that, based on an interpolation of the
Scriptures, found in the prayer for the dedication of the water in
the Anglican Office of Baptism: "Thanks unto thee . . . for that
thy dearly beloved Son Jesus Christ, for the forgiveness of our sins,
did shed out of his most precious side both water and blood. . . ."[3]
In short, let us not be saying officially in prayer what obviously we

[3] Happily, the revision of these particular items has been recommended
tentatively by the Standing Liturgical Commission of the Episcopal Church.

do not mean—in violation of the venerable and sound principle *lex orandi est lex credendi*.

As for ceremonies, we should eliminate ones which have no meaning to communicate, such as the solemn extinguishing of candles at the end of a service, the congregation kneeling expectantly until the last one is extinguished and then rising en masse on a swell of the organ. Such a ceremony might have a significant meaning for Zoroastrians; but we are not fire-worshipers.

2. *Salvaging.* As for doctrine, Predestination and Election afford a useful example. The flat statement of these doctrines is intolerable, as we have seen. On the other hand, there is a motif behind these doctrines which is illuminating with regard to man's relationship to God: all men are called to salvation, and will be "elected" therefor if they will "run"; when one has come into the new life one then knows experientially that God was there first, it being of His very nature to wish this outcome, and hence He has "predestined" the response (the now obscure phrase "prevenient grace" similarly reflects a genuine truth). Thus salvaged, even "double predestination" expresses a truth, as long as it is not applied oversimply to distinguish one group of men from another, but rather to factors in the lives of each individual: all that is good in *each* man is eternally endorsed and all that is evil is eternally condemned.

As for prayers, certain concepts can focus the imagination on particular aspects of God. The imagery of angels (about which we factually know *nothing*) can represent God's versatility and ever-presence in action; however, we should find words to break the flat literalness of, for example, the Anglican Collect for Michaelmas: "O everlasting God, who hast ordained and constituted the services of Angels and men in a wonderful order; Mercifully grant, that as thy holy Angels always do thee service in heaven, so, by thy appointment, they may succour and defend us on earth. . . ."[4] And if there is point to the narrative about the Holy Innocents (I will confess that I have never precisely sensed what the eternal

[4] Book of Common Prayer, p. 251.

significance is; and most of us dread when, every six or seven years, this Feast falls on a Sunday and hence calls for a sermon), we should seek to express more meaning than is carried by the Collect for the day: "O Almighty God, who out of the mouths of babes and sucklings hast ordained strength, and madest infants to glorify thee by their deaths; Mortify and kill all vices in us, etc." A radical salvaging operation is obviously needed here.

3. *Preservation intact, with interpretation.* The revision of the traditional Creeds is simply regarded by most Christians as outside the realm of possibility. But as St. Thomas Aquinas reminded us, you cannot deny possibility in the face of actuality, and a successful actuality is the Statement of Faith of the United Church of Christ set forth at the close of the preceding chapter. But this came in the context of, and with the enthusiasm generated by, a significant step in Christian unity: the merger of the Evangelical and Reformed Church (a previous union) and the Congregational Christian Churches (likewise), and each of the uniting Churches has been very much in the free-church tradition. In the Churches with fixed liturgies, rewriting or revision of the Creeds in the foreseeable future is unlikely—the task not being in fact impossible (as has already been established) but politically unlikely, in the light of the conservatism about such matters in Churches of this type—no matter how liberal they may be in other ways.

Thus if it is assumed that there will continue in use such phrases as "came down from Heaven," "descended into Hell," "ascended into Heaven," "of one substance with the Father," and "proceedeth from the Father and the Son"—each of which represents (however inadequately) a valid truth—then what is needed is persistent effort at translation by preaching, teaching, and writing.

The same is also true of the Ten Commandments, which are doubtless here to stay—though, as we have seen, they are not absolutes, nor do they come near to covering the realm of moral obligation. Clear teaching about their origin and context and about the full claim expressed in the *Sh'ma Israel*, with ample and varied *ad hoc* illustrations of the application of the Claim, can prevent the distorted view of ethics which would come from the repeated reading of the Commandments without interpretation.

This same approach—preservation with interpretation—applies to many of the customary externals of worship, which can be beautiful and meaningful in our time, provided there is candor about the historical development of these various items so that they are not viewed as absolutes. For example, candles in the sanctuary are fine; but, as the Bishop who ordained me, Dr. Angus Dun, once pointed out at a meeting of a low-church society: "Man is not saved by candles, nor by *no* candles either." And in the field of polity the historic episcopate, though not to be exalted in terms of ecclesiastical exclusivism, nevertheless can be an impressive witness to the organic continuity of the Church (see App. B, ¶ 7). Self-serving as this comment may seem to be, abolition is not called for, but careful teaching informed by historical perspective.

A telling illustration is the question of the right place today of the biblical passages about the Virgin Birth. Just as "the sabbath was made for man, and not man for the sabbath" (Mark 2:27, RSV), so too the status to be afforded a tradition should be determined with consideration for the groups of people sought to be reached by the gospel. For generations, many intelligent people have been put off from Christianity by the Church's apparently absolute proclamation of the Virgin Birth narratives as both history and dogma. On the other hand, many others have felt seriously threatened whenever the historical truth of the narratives has been questioned or whenever the importance of the Virgin Birth has been minimized. Further, in any era, with any conceptual or semantic equipment, it is difficult to devise propositions or images which adequately carry the paradox of Who Jesus Christ is; that is, a particular man in Whom the fullness of God dwelt and acted. We can see this by examining some of the conventional attempts: The *logos* approach in John is abstract for most people; the nature-substance-person categories of fifth-century Greek philosophy likewise—and are even more a hindrance to communication than the *logos* format; the Messianic category presupposes a considerable knowledge of—and feeling for—historic Jewish thought. By far more popular and more universally useful for communication has been the Virgin Birth image, and it does not appear that we are likely to devise a better one.

What is needed, then, is candor about the difficulties in holding these narratives to be historical, which arise from the text of the New Testament books themselves,[5] and boldness in making clear that their historical truth could hardly be regarded as an essential of the Faith, and at the same time affirmative use of the image liturgically and in the folk activities which surround the Christmas season.

Some who would favor the general process of demythologization and remythologization hold, in regard to this particular image, that it is in fact not a suitable one in that the picture compromises the true humanity of Jesus. But this is a form of literalness in reverse. True, if the stories are pressed to their full implications, One without a human father—but rather a "divine" One—is not a true man; yet myths like parables are not to be pushed to their full implications but are to be left as over-all images of paradoxical truth.

Yet, it must be granted that good Christian people can reasonably disagree as to the utility of any of these secondary matters and yet agree wholeheartedly as to the task that is before the Church in this and every age: to speak to the world in Christian candor, according to our lights, in faithfulness to the essentials

[5] In brief: The earliest Christian writings (the Epistles of Paul and the Gospel of Mark) do not mention the Virgin Birth; in fact Paul asserts that Jesus was "born of a woman under the law." The notion is not included in the summaries of the Gospel by Paul or in the kerygmatic sermons reported in Acts. It finds no place in the more sophisticated expression of Christian belief and experience which forms the Fourth Gospel. The narratives are found in Matthew and Luke, but would appear to represent a late stratum of tradition, since they contradict the genealogies in the same two Gospels; these, which were intended to satisfy potential Jewish converts that Jesus was of the blood lineage of David (thought to be essential to Messiahship), lead down to Joseph.

of the Catholic Faith, by way of ideas, words, forms, and images that illumine rather than obfuscate. Fundamental to the fulfillment of this task is the recognition of the distinction between the treasure and the vessels—not only in the interest of communication but for a reason basic to true religion: *that the excellency of the power may be of God, and not of us.*

APPENDIX A

"TRINITY IN UNITY": REMARRIAGE IN THE EPISCOPAL CHURCH

The canon law on remarriage was totally revised at the 1946 General Convention of the Protestant Episcopal Church—and ever since has been interpreted in three different ways.

The portion of the Canon which provides the basis for judgment reads as follows:

> . . . The Bishop or Ecclesiastical authority shall take care that his or its judgment is based upon and conforms to the doctrine of this Church, that marriage is a physical, spiritual, and mystical union of a man and woman created by their mutual consent of heart, mind, and will thereto, and is a Holy Estate instituted of God and is *in intention* lifelong; *but when* any of the facts set forth in Canon 17, §2(b) [which lists the impediments to matrimony], are shown *to exist or to have existed* which manifestly establish that no marriage bond as the same is recognized by this Church exists, the same may be declared by proper authority. . . .[1]

First, as to nullity, it should be noted (from the words "to exist or to have existed" italicized above) that facts which would have been an impediment to a marriage had they arisen before the marriage may now serve as a basis for the declaration of the right to remarry even though they arose after the marriage began. This new basis for a favorable judgment is commonly called "extended nullity."

Second, the wording allows a favorable judgment on a basis of the "spiritual death" of the marriage. The separate character of this remedy is made clear by (*a*) the fact that the provision for the declaration of nullity in Canon 18, §2(b), is not stated as a

[1] Canon 18, §2(b). Italics added.

condition to the episcopal judgment, but is stated *disjunctively* (it is introduced by the words "but when" and not the word, "if"); and (*b*) the fact that the basis of the Bishop's judgment is declared to be the teaching that "marriage is a physical, spiritual, and mystical union of a man and woman created by their mutual consent of heart, mind, and will thereto [which under certain circumstances can have ceased to exist] and is *in intention* life long. Had the Church intended in this revised Canon to proclaim an ontological, as contrasted with an existential, view of the marriage bond (see pp. 46f.), it could very well have left out the crucial words, "in intention."

But, in fact, three different interpretations of the Canon obtain in the various dioceses: (*a*) strict nullity only, (*b*) extended nullity and (*c*) spiritual death + the declaration of nullity in appropriate cases.

Another incongruity has developed in this field: One of the principles of the Reformation was the equality of the moral law as to the laity and the clergy, whether they are "religious" (i.e., under vow in an Order) or "secular"—clergy or laymen. Nevertheless, though the canon law of our Church makes no distinction between clergy and laity as to eligibility for application for remarriage,[2] and though a determined attempt at the General Convention of 1958 to permit applications only from the laity failed of adoption (thus providing an interpretation reinforcing the plain words of the Canon: namely, that it indeed applies to clergy and laity alike), some bishops refuse absolutely to receive an application for remarriage from a clergyman; some refuse to receive as applicants for postulancy for Holy Orders those who have had a remarriage (even though the marriage was authorized by the Church and solemnized by a priest of the Church); some bishops refuse to receive into their dioceses any priest who has had two marriages—regardless of the canonical correctness of the second marriage; and other bishops do not draw any such absolute distinctions.

[2] See Canon 18, §1.

APPENDIX B

ON CERTAIN RELATIVITIES
IN CULT AND POLITY

1. Unsophisticated finalization can be seen in certain aspects of the ceremonial development of the Churches of the Anglican Communion since the beginning of the Oxford Movement in the nineteenth century. Early Anglo-Catholics, eager to have their services look more "Catholic" (as though true Catholicity depended upon the ceremonial) turned for liturgical norms to the most conspicuous Catholic body in Europe, namely, the Roman Catholic Church (whose liturgical practice was, incidentally, at about its lowest ebb at that time). This was the norm, the "right" way the Eucharist should be celebrated. To the degree that the Anglican rite of 1662 did not lend itself to the Western Use of the Roman Church, the Anglo–Catholics often altered their Liturgy to conform more closely to the Latin rite. Or to the degree that, owing to fear of the laity they did not "go whole hog," they regarded their own reticence as compromise (though perhaps a necessary one), and patiently or impatiently awaited the time that by "sound teaching" the laity would be more ready to go along.

However, further research into the pre-Reformation ceremonial of *Ecclesia Anglicana,* especially the predominant rite of the late medieval period, namely, that of Sarum (Salisbury) stimulated a new movement for the restoration of the "English rite" (in contrast to the "Western rite"). This group, though "Catholic-minded," has been loyal to the 1662 Prayer Book (or other authorized Prayer Books). But for many the ceremonial usages of

Sarum were absolute, *the* "right way." (Hence the taunt of the "Western Use" devotees: Sarum was called the "British Museum" use.) Then along came the Liturgical Movement (shared concurrently with the Roman Catholic Church, and to a lesser degree with other Churches)—an effort to revive certain early Church practices, in order to increase the participation of the laity and to give more emphasis to the relationship of the Eucharist to daily life and social concern, etc.

Though the author is part of this movement (with some predilections for Sarum, in an eclectic spirit), he will admit that in it, too, there is a tendency to speak of certain early Church customs as "the right way": in other words, to absolutize the historically conditioned. It is true that these revived usages better involve—and speak to—the congregation. Recognizing better ways to communicate is one thing; but the frequent references, in the literature and preaching on this subject, to "the early Church" (just which century is generally not specified) implies the first premise of an unstated syllogism, namely, that that which is earlier is automatically better, or, rather, that the absolute norm for the measuring of practices in any other century is what was done in the early Church. On what basis, either empirical or logical, can we support such canonization of the practices of a given period of early Church history, any more than of fifteenth-century Sarum? Is there any more basis for this premise than there is for the premise that whatever is *later* is better (an axiom to which we have become accustomed in a culture dominated by the doctrine of "inevitable progress")?

2. Let us turn from ceremonies to the supposed "essential" elements in the Eucharist. The more extensive the historical investigation of early liturgies, the less are we able to affirm this or that is an "essential." What *is* "the heart of the matter"? For a long time Anglo-Catholics thought that the Words of Institution represented the actual "moment" of Consecration (and their ceremonial use suitably was in accord with this teaching). Meanwhile, a school of thought among eucharistic-centered and, in general, "high" churchmen, insisted that the Invocation of the

Holy Spirit represented the "moment" of Consecration (and a proper Sarum "profound bow" was to be executed at the end of this paragraph of the Canon). Then at the Lambeth Conference of 1958 we learned in effect that neither school of thought was right, that the entire thanksgiving action (from the *Sursum corda* on) consecrated, on the ground that it is thankful dedication, not formula, that makes holy. Again, I confess a bias for this latter position; it underlies the ceremonial directions in my Diocesan Customary (it is interesting that some Roman Catholic liturgiologists are now urging it in contrast to the present centering of the ceremonial on the Words of Institution); yet to absolutize this position one would have to overlook long-standing support of the other two alternatives in various places and in various Churches throughout Christian history.

A related example: The provision until recently in the canon law of our Church which allowed the ordination of a non-Episcopal minister without withdrawing him from the fellowship of his own Church,[1] while not requiring of the ordinand a commitment to use our form of Eucharist, did set down what was regarded as the essentials of a Eucharist, requiring that these be included in any celebration he undertook. Since this was drafted at a particular time in history, it naturally reflected our particular knowledge at the time, and the minimum requirements thus included the Words of Institution and an Invocation. We have since learned that in certain early liturgies, e.g., the Rite of Hippolytus, neither of these appeared; and yet we are not prepared to declare that celebrations in the early Church were invalid. This is not to say that these features of the service are not desirable or meaningful, but this historical information does indicate that even these cannot be called *essential*.

3. Another example of unfounded rigidities in the field of Cult can be found in the contention (now somewhat subsided) in our Communion between those who believe in two sacraments and those who believe in seven. Even the two-sacrament contenders have granted that there is a place, in one form or another, for what

[1] Canon 36, §§ 1-3 (before its amendment in 1961).

seven-sacrament people have regarded as the other five sacraments, and the latter have been willing to concede the greater importance of the two rites to which the low churchmen limited the word "sacrament"; but still the two–seven distinction has seemed by members of each group something essential enough to fight over. The scars have been somewhat healed by a degree of semantic care (e.g., in our Church's officially published textbook on doctrine, after the sections on Baptism and Holy Communion is a third heading, "Other Sacramental Rites"[2]), and through the growing conviction (strengthened by the writings of the late Archbishop William Temple) that we are in a "sacramental universe," in which all kinds of relationships are sacramental.

4. That those who would absolutize the *number* of sacraments or the meaning and content of particular sacramental rites have overlooked the history of these matters, is manifest. Take, for example, Confirmation. After a brief period in the early Church when new converts were baptized and chrismated by the bishop, these actions were done (albeit with oil which the bishop had blessed) by the local presbyter. It was only later, and in the Western Church only, that bishops began to confirm separately from baptism and at an older age, and still later that the theory was developed that Confirmation represented the conscious adult acceptance of baptismal vows (something obviously impossible in the case of infants chrismated at the time of their baptism). Now many talk about it as lay ordination. A comparison of the words of the Prayer Book Office of Confirmation and those of Holy Baptism, now that the two are separated, indicate that much more fulsome language is used about the conferring of the Holy Spirit in Baptism than is used in Confirmation. Further, the plethora of scholarship which has centered on the "initiatory rites" leave us in doubt as to what precisely Confirmation is. When it comes to such questions of Church unity as the degree of Anglican intercommunion with a Church like the Church of South India, a number of Episcopalians insist that Confirmation is an absolute

---

[2] J. A. Pike and N. Pittenger, *The Faith of the Church* (The Church's Teaching Series; New York: Seabury Press, 1951), Chap. X.

"must,"[3] though as has been suggested, the history of the rite and of its meaning and usage show the contingent character of it.

5. The same is true of the sacrament/sacramental rite of Unction. For centuries before the Reformation it was "Extreme Unction," as a part of the last rites. At the Reformation it was abolished, in England and in the Continental Reformed Churches, because the Reformers could find no biblical basis for last rites. However, in modern times a change has come. Provision has been made in the Prayer Books of various Provinces of the Anglican Communion[4] for laying on of hands and the anointing of the sick, restoring it as described in the Epistle of James—as a sacramental rite of healing, whether the patient is *in extremis* or not. Likewise this restoration has just occurred in the Roman Catholic Church.[5] The point is that it is difficult to absolutize a sacramental rite which until recently all the Western Churches had lacked, in its biblical import, since the days of the early Church.

6. As to the "Sacrament of Penance," in the early Church the general pattern was (*a*) direct confession to God, (*b*) a General Confession and Absolution in the service (the remnant of this remains even in the Roman rite, in the *preparatio* of the Mass—though now participated in by only the priest and acolytes), and (*c*) excommunication and restoration in the case of major sins causing scandal. In the Western Church, from the early Middle Ages, private confession for "mortal sin" was made *essential* (it always existed before as a voluntary opportunity for persons burdened with a sense of guilt after having "taken the matter up" with God). At the Reformation, compulsory private confession was abolished, but Anglican and Lutheran traditions explicitly (and other traditions implicitly—via pastoral counseling) left private confession as a voluntary opportunity; public confes-

---

[3] These won the day at the Episcopal General Convention of 1961, where it was provided C.S.I. members may receive Communion with us only when confirmed—this in a Church in which in relatively few parishes would an American Presbyterian in practice be denied Communion.

[4] E.g., American Book of Common Prayer, p. 320.

[5] Constitution on the Liturgy (Vatican Council II, 1963), § 73.

sion was made really "public"—the "General Confession" in the Eucharist being brought back to the people; and excommunication and restoration were retained.[6] One might be inclined to say that these are merely procedural changes; but not at all—considering the supposed relationship of private confession to eternal destiny (let alone to temporal peace of mind). Again, in the light of the changes throughout history, where is the permanence of this supposed absolute?

7. Absolutist notions have also entered into the matter of what ministers may properly celebrate the sacraments. In some Churches this function is limited to bishops in the historic succession and priests and deacons ordained by them (except in the case of laymen baptizing in an emergency). This can be justified pragmatically for our Church; but there are those who infer from this rule that all sacraments celebrated by other Christian ministers are invalid. As to this matter in our Church, three views are permissible in regard to the significance of episcopal ordination:

a. It is *de bene esse*, i.e., for the well-being of the Church: in short, a "good idea."

b. It is *de plene esse*, i.e., for the fullness of the Church: recognition of the fact that it has existed from the earliest times and is extant in by far the largest percentage of Christianity today, and that since it is plausible to assume that God has been guiding the Church in such a conspicuous and continuing development, it should be a part of any contemplated united Church (it is virtually taken for granted in most current unity proposals that it will be); but the lack of it, due to historical circumstances, does not "invalidate" the ministry and sacraments outside of this particular historic succession.

c. It is *de esse*, i.e., essential for valid ministry and sacraments.

[6] See e.g., the rubrics on pp. 84-85, Book of Common Prayer, and Canon 16, §§ 5 and 6.

APPENDIX C

ON CHRISTOLOGICAL HERESIES

As has been explained in Chapter III, the Church has almost always made its definitions in terms of particular distortions or apparent distortions. In declaring heretical certain attempts at Christological explanation, the Church seems to have been right. Hence any attempt in our day to explain the fact of Jesus Christ ought to be checked against the decisions of the Councils against the principal hetero-orthodox attempts of the past. If the position taken in Chapter VIII on Christology should concur with one or another of the well-established heresies, then at the least it should be subjected to particularly careful examination. This is, of course, equally true if what is said appears to be a new heresy. But this is unlikely since a large number of thoughtful Christians in the early centuries of Christendom devoted themselves to seeking to state a doctrine of Christ, and the heresy-hunters of the past were very avid indeed in sifting those statements. Thus it is not certain that new heresies in the field of Christology could be contrived—even if one were bent on so doing. Thus we will briefly undertake these comparisons.

Adoptionism. This view affirms that Jesus was so sound and good as a man that God chose Him as His Son and as the Messiah. But the thesis here proposed presupposes that God does not make *particular* decisions—and did not in the Incarnation or otherwise.

Arianism. This view declares that Jesus Christ is a sub-God created by God. But under the view here taken the Ultimate Ground, in its complete depth and breadth already present universally, visibly enters history in terms of a particular human being. Any limitations on this manifestation of the only God is in the human vehicle and human perception of this manifestation, not in Him who is thus manifested.

Appolinarianism. Under this view Jesus = God, but lacks a full human nature. But the approach of this emphasizes Jesus' individual manhood (including freedom of choice) while affirming that Ultimate Ground is, without reservation, in Him. The emphasis on the reality of the life, death, and Resurrection of the historical, human Jesus would also make the view here developed far from *Gnosticism* or *Docetism.*

Nestorianism. Here Jesus is God + man, two persons in one. The assertion in this work that the presence of the Ultimate Ground is universal and that He is not a Being beside other beings would belie any implication that we are talking about two separate Persons in Jesus.

Monophysitism. This view affirms readily enough that Jesus is one person but goes on to say that He has only one "nature"—a mixed divine and human nature: in short, half God + half man. But, as has been asserted, Jesus is a real, i.e., a whole, man, and in Him the full God is expressed and known.

Monothelitism. Here Jesus is one person, with two "natures," but with only one will. But the position in Chapter VIII puts particular stress on the freedom of Jesus as man to accept or to decline the Messianic role.

Not, strictly speaking, a Christological heresy, since it bears on the nature of the Trinity, is *Sabellianism,* or *Modalist Monarchianism.* Under this view Father, Son, and Holy Spirit are simply a succession of modes or operations of God. However, the pages above affirm that God is fully in all that the Church has affirmed about each of the three "Persons," and that what is thus expressed is integral to His nature.

APPENDIX D. LITURGICAL REFORM TOWARD RELEVANT CONTINUITY

The following illustrates some aspects of the Liturgical Movement as adopted in many Roman Catholic and Anglican Churches (as well as in some others, such as the chapel in the French Reformed Monastery at Taizé):

	THE TEACHING	THE CONVENTIONAL REMNANT	THE NEW—BUT ANCIENT
The Gospel Procession (during the Gradual—the hymn or psalm after the Epistle)	The Gospel is to be taken to the world—is on the move.	An acolyte moves the missal (altar service book) from one side of the altar to the other, from which side of the Gospel is read.	The deacon/gospeller goes with the Book of the Gospels in procession (in larger places accompanied by cross and torches) to a point near the congregation.
The Offertory Procession	The offering to God—through tokens of our work and joy—of ourselves	An acolyte brings the bread and wine from the credence table in the sanctuary to the celebrant at the altar; laymen collect the alms and [Anglican] bring them to the celebrant for offering.	After the collection of the alms, the alms bearers are joined by oblation bearers who have taken the bread and the wine from a credence table at the entry of the nave (the location identifying them with the people, and all together go forward to the Altar for the Offertory, remaining there [Anglican] for the Prayer for the Church.
The Pax (anciently called "the Kiss of Peace")	Our fellowship in the Faith; reconciliation between men	After the Fraction (the breaking of the bread) the celebrant says or sings: "The peace of the Lord be always with you." *Response:* "And with thy spirit."	After the Fraction [thus stressing the fellowship note] or after the Offertory Sentences [stressing the reconciliation note: cf. Matt. 5:23-24] the celebrant greets the deacons with a handshake and the salutation (see col. 3); they greet others in the sanctuary and choir and representative laymen, who in turn take the Pax to the congregation (the person at the end of the pew extending the Pax to his neighbor, and so on). Each person greeted says the Response.

INDEX OF NAMES AND SUBJECTS

Entries in boldface type indicate the principal discussion of the topic.

Abolitionists, 38
Abraham, 28, 63, 127
Absolutism, 10 f., 23–30, 31 n., 37 f., 41 f., 49–54, 57 f., 85 f., 134, 145–150
"Act of God," 82
Adam, 74 f., 77, 96
Adoptionism, 52, 151
Africa, 18, 30, 45, 110, 123
Agnosticism, 14, 67, 152
Alcoholics Anonymous, 77
Alcoholism, 59, 61, 65 f., 71, 78, 80 f., 93 f.
Angels, 83 f., 137
Anglicanism, 7, 12 n., 28, 30 f., 38, 40 f., 44 f., 47 f., 49 n., 52 ff., 72, 92, 101, 104 f., 133 n., 136 f., 143 ff., 153
Anglo-Catholicism, 30, 145 f.
Anglo-Saxon law, 45, 82
Annulment, ecclesiastical, 27, 47, 143 f.
Anxiety, 75, 77
Apartheid, 30 n.
Apocrypha, the, 120, 125
Apollinarianism, 52, 152
Apologetics, 8 f., 30 n.
Apostolic succession, *see* Succession, historic
Apostles' Creed, 20, 31, 35, 125
Aquinas, St. Thomas, 20, 33 f., 88, 138
Aristotle, 20, 34
Arius, Arianism, 31 f., 151 f.
Art and iconography, Christian, 39
Articles of Religion, 30
Ascension, the, 36, 77, 127 f.
Assumption of Mary, doctrine, 29
Athanasian Creed, 31, 34 f.
Atonement, the, 35, 118
Augsburg Confession, 29

Augustine, St., 48 n., 61 f., 69

Bailey, D. S., *Sexual Relation in Christian Thought,* 48 n.
Baptism, 12, 45, 53, 57, 64, 68 f., 73, 75, 77, 136, 148, 150
Baptist Churches, 53
Bayne, S., *Christian Living,* 49 n.
Belief, 9–12, **13 ff.**, 28, 62–65, 69 f., 75, 79 f., 83–85, 87–89, 91, 101, 114, 129 f.; act of will, 19 f., 73; knowledge in, 19–21; loss of faith, 59–60; reasons for lack of, *see* Roadblocks to faith; relation to experience, 19, 21 f., 65; trust, 19; universality of, 15 f.; what belief is not, 17 f.
Bible, Holy, 25 ff., 31 n., 36, 38, 50, 54–56, 124, 126, 135 f.; canon of Scripture, 28 f.; Church prior to, 28; creed of the fundamentalist, 31 n.; interpretation of, 25–29, 124; Lectionary, 135 f.; *New English Bible, The,* 133; New Testament, 28, 74, 108, 120, 125, 127 f., 140; not final, 29; Old Testament, 28, 120, 125, 127
Bibliolatry, 25 ff.
Birth control, 26 f., **41 ff.**
Bishop of Woolwich, *see* Robinson, J. A. T.
Bishops, 30, 55 f., 143 f., 148, 150
Body of Christ, the, 73, 77
Book of Common Prayer, 31, 33, 36, 48, 55, 73 f., 77, 87, 89, 92, 95 n., 96, 98, 128, 136–38, 145, 148

Break-through of God in Christ, *see* Incarnation
Buber, Martin, 124
Bull *Apostolicae Curae,* 54
Bunyan, John, 69, 72

Cahn, E., *The Moral Decision,* 50 n.
California, 8, 135
Canon law, 27, 143 f., 147
Capital punishment, 41
Casserly, J. V. Langmead, *The Christian in Philosophy,* 121
Catechism, 40
Celibacy, 46 n., 49
Change, 10, 38–41, 47–50, 60–62, 64 f., 72, 88–90, 99, 132–38
Christology, 12, 30–32, **108 ff.** 120 ff., 138 f., 151 f.
Church, the, 9 f., 14, 24, 28–30, 38 f., 51, 55–58, 67 f., 72, 77, 89, 97, 109, 118, 121 f., 124
Church of South India, 53, 56 n., 148–49
Churchill, Sir Winston, 76
Claim, the, 28, 94–97, 109 f., 113, 139
Codes, 11 f., **37 ff.**, 63, 113, 131
Commandment, First Great, 11
Commandments, the Ten, 37, **39 ff.**, 94, 138 f.; the two Great, 38
Commitment, 20 f.
Communication, 32, 121–123, 131–41
Communion of Saints, 119
Compulsions, 81, 92 f., 97
Conditioning, *see* Social conditioning
Confession, private and public, 54, 95 f., 149 f.
Confessions of Faith, 29 f., 31 n., 36

Confirmation, 54, 57, 69, 71, 148

Congregationalists, the Congregational Churches, 38, 138

Constantine, Emperor, 89

Continuity, 132–34, 153

Consubstantiation, 34

Conversion, 45 f., 60 ff., 68 f., 72 f., 75 f., 124

Copernicus, 111

Councils of the Church, 25, 29–30, 124 f.

Cranmer, Archbishop, 33

Creed of Pius IV, 31 n.

Creeds, 12, **24 ff.**, 36 f., 63, 126, 129–131, 138; see also the various Creeds by name

Cross, the, 63 ff., 73–75, 77 f., 85, 91, 100, 107, 110, 113, 116 ff., 127

Cult, 37, **51 ff.**, 63, 129, 131, 145 ff.; see also Polity, Worship

Cushing, Richard Cardinal, 123

Damnation, see Salvation

David, 109, 140 n.

Dead Sea Scrolls, 109

Dearmer, Dr. Percy, 112

Death, 64, 82 f., 92

Death of Christ, see Cross, the

Decisions, societal and individual, 41, 61, 69, 75 f., 80–82, 84, 92–94

Deductive reasoning, 42–44

Devil, the demonic, 66, 76, 83 f., 118

Divorce, 27 n., 46 f., 143 f.

Docetism, 152

Donne, John, 75

Dun, Dr. Angus, 139

Eastern Orthodox Church, 46, 125

Ecclesiastical structure, see Polity

Ecclesiolatry, 29

Economic systems, 42, 85

Edenic myth, 27, 74 f., 84, 96

Election, see Predestination

Emotion, role of, 15, 20, 59, 71, 78

Encyclical *Pacem in Terris,* 42 n.

English rite, 145

Ennui, meaninglessness, 15, 59–61, 78

Episcopal, see Anglicanism

Eschatology, 89, 109

Essenes, 109

Essentia, 121 f.

Essentials vs. nonessentials, 8 f., 23 f., 54 f., 57 f., 67, 124 f., 128, 140 f., 146 ff.

Eternal life, 35, 59, 67, 83, 85, 88, 91, 113, 116, 118 f., 150

Ethics, 11 f., 14, 23 f., 37 ff., 43, 45, 49 f.; "situational," 11; see also Code, Sin

Eucharist, the, 12, 33 f., 48, 53 f., 57, 64, 72, 73 n., 77, 107, 136, 145–150

Evangelical and Reformed Church, 138

Evangelicals, 38

Evil, the problem of, 75, **78 ff.**, 85–87, 94, 136

Evolution, 80, 86, 100, 126 f.

Exclusivism, 56, 67 f.

Excommunication, 149

Existence of God, 16, 20

Existentialism, existential, 10 ff., 46, 49, 79, 90, 93, 102, 107, 125, 128 f., 144

Exodus, the, 63, 101, 105 f., 127

Faith, see Belief

Faith, the, the Catholic Faith, 12, 24, 28, 32, 52, 57, 65, 69–71, 108 f., 111, 124, 139–41

Fall of man, see Original Sin

Father-figure, 14

Fathers of the Church, 28, 32, 48, 122; see also Councils of the Church

Feast, of Easter, 63; of the Holy Innocents, 137 f.; of Michaelmas, 137; of the Resurrection (Sunday), 40; of Unleavened Bread, 54

Filioque clause, 125

Fourth Lateran Council, 33

Fox, George, 69

Freedom, 62, 76, 80–84, 90, 92 f., 95 f., 102, 114

Freud, Freudian, 14, 61, 126, 128 f.

Friends Home Service Committee, *Towards a Christian View of Sex,* 49 n.

Fundamentalism, biblical, **25 ff.**, 31, 54; creedal, 31 n., 35

Gnosticism, 67, 126

God, as Absolute, 85 f., 134; Actor, 73, 100, 108, 110, 113 f.; Claimant, 10, 94, 97, 131; Creator, 86, 90, 125 ff.; eternal, 63, 101, 111, 127; Evolver and Sustainer, 126 f.; Giver of life, 125; Goodness, 83–87, 109, 118, 128; Grace, 101, 106; Guide, 106; Healer, 106, 127; Holy Spirit, 72 f., 98, 120 ff., 125 f.; infinite, 100; Judge, 97, 101, 128; Justice, 100, 103 f., 110; Love, 61, 100 f., 103, 105, 110, 113; natural, 100, 109, 114; omnipotent, 80, 85–87; omnipresent, 100, 106 f., 110, 128; perfect, 94; personal, 102 f.; Power, 91, 100 f., 103 f., 106 f., 110, 113; Purpose, 105; Redeemer, 10, 90, 99, 100, 110, 113, 127; Response, 108; Revealer, 63 f., 85, 100 f., 103, 109 f., 112, 113–15, 128; Source, 19, 99, 104 f., 112 f., 127; "supernatural," 100, 114; Ultimate Ground, 10, 19, 24, 32,

64 f., 69, 77, 86, 9 f., 94, **99 ff.**, 104, 106, 108, 112–14, 119, 121, 127 f., 131, 134, 151; unchangeable, 98 f., 108, 127; unconditioned, 99, 102, 104, 107; unfailing, 107; universal, 69, 108; wholly Other, 100
Golden Rule, 37
Good, goodness, 75 f., 85, **88–91**, 94, 97, 109 f., 118, 134; see also God as Goodness
Gospel, see Faith, the, the Catholic Faith
Gospel Procession, 133 n., 153
Government, Church, see Polity
Glossolalia, 67
Grace, 48, 56 f., 85, 90, 97, 101, 106 f., 137
Greek way of thinking, 35, 120 ff., 140 f.
Groups, 76 f., 90, 106
Guilt, 62, 95 f.

Hebrew way of thinking, 35, 120
Heidelberg Confession, 29
Henry VIII, 27
Heresy, 7, 9, 24, 31, 67, 108, 121, 151 f.; see also singly, by name—Arianism, etc.
Hippolytus, Rite of, 147
Historical conditioning, see Social conditioning
Historismus, history of ideas, 11, 43
Hitler, 76
Holy Communion, see Eucharist, the
Holy Orders, 54 f., 144, 147, 150
Holy Spirit, see God as Holy Spirit
Homoiousion, homoousion, 32
Honest to God, J. A. T. Robinson, 7–9
Honest to God Debate, The, D. Edwards and J. A. T. Robinson, eds., 7 n.

Hosea, 127
House of Bishops, Pastoral Letter (1958), 104 f.
Humanism, 89
Hymns, 28, 52 f., 63, 74, 112
Hypostasis, 34, 121 f.

Identification, 70, 73, 75, 77
Idolatry, 23–25, 28, 33 f., 51
Impediments to matrimony, 27, 47, 143
Incarnation, the, 36, **108 ff.,** 127; see also Christology
Indifference, religious, 13 ff.
Inductive reasoning, 42–44
Infallibility, 23, 25, 29, 41, 55
Integration, personal, 16, 60 f., 66
Interpretation of Scripture, 25–29, 124, 138–41
is and *ought* dynamic, 88–90
Isaac, 63, 127
Islamic evangelism, 123
Israel, Israelites, 28, 100, 105, 111, 113 f., 116 f., 135

Jacob, 63
James, St., 124, Epistle of, 149
James, William, *The Varieties of Religious Experience,* 58, 59, 69 f., 72 f.
Jefferson, Thomas, *The Jefferson Bible,* 37
Jerome, St., 48 n.
Jewish-Christian community, early, 40, 61, 120
John, St., 124; Gospel according to, 22
John of Damascus, St., 63
Joseph, son of Jacob, 127
Joseph (Holy Family), 140 n.
Judaism, 28, 39 f., 62 f., 77, 105, 109, 117, 120, 124
Judeo-Christian tradition, 18 f., 82, 87 f.

Judgment, 50, 77, 89, 93 f., 99, 101, **104 f.,** 128
Justification, 133 f.

kairos, 113
Katherine of Aragon, 27
Kierkegaard, Søren, 19, 131
Killing, 40 f.
Kingdom of God, 77, 88 f., 91, 109, 116, 127
Knox, Msgr. Ronald, translation of the Bible, 133
Krumm, J. M., co-author of *Roadblocks to Faith,* 23 n.

Lambeth Conference, 1920, 41; 1958, 41, 45, 49 n., 147
Last Supper, 54
Law, canon, 27, 143 f., 147; civil and criminal, 50, 92 f.; see also Claim, the; Commandments
"Leap of faith," 19–21, 27 f., 44
Lecomte du Noüy, Pierre, 80
Lectionary, 135 f.
Leo XIII, Pope, 54
Lewis, C. S., *The Screwtape Letters,* 84
Liberalism, 34
Liturgical Movement, 53, 133, 146, 153
Liturgy, see Worship
Logic, 16–19, 50, 75 f.; axioms, assumptions, premises, 15 ff., 43 f.; syllogisms, 17 f., 43 f.; see also Deductive reasoning, Inductive reasoning, Plausibility
Lord's Supper, see Eucharist, the
Love, 77, 90, 94, 97; see also God as Love
Lowrie, Dr. Walter, 55 f.; in *Dr. Lowrie of Princeton and Rome,* H. Johnson, ed., 56 n.
Lunn and Lean, *The New Morality,* 49 n.

Luther, Martin, 62, 69
Lutheran Church, Lutheranism, 29, 34, 149 f.

Maccabees, the, 89
Mammon, 16
Man, doctrine of, 75 ff., 81, 84
Manicheanism, 83
Marcion, Marcionism, 62 f., 127 n.
Marriage, 46 ff., 94 f., 143 f.; impediments to matrimony, 27, 47, 143 f.; intention in, 143 f.; see also Birth control
Martyrs, Christian, 89, 117
Mass, the, see Eucharist
McNaughton's Case, 92 f.
Messiah, messianic, 61, 77, 140 n.
Methodist Church, 39
Methodology, 10 ff.
Mission, 77, 124
Modalism, 125 n., 152
Moments I and/or II, 58 ff., 69 f., 74, 77–79, 98, 100 f., 109, 118
Monogamy, 45
Monophysitism, 152
Monotheism, 16, 83 f., 94, 120 f., 123
Morals, see Ethics
Mores, 9, 23, 113; vs. morals, 23
Moses, 105
Murder, 40 f.
Muslims, 123 f.
Mystical union, 74
Mysticism, 67, 76
Myth, mythological, 27 74 f., 86, 124, 131 f., 140

Name of God, 39 f.
National Council of Churches, 39
Natural law, 11, 38, 41 ff., 50
Nestorianism, 152
Newman, Cardinal, 74
Nicene Creed, 31, 35, 114 f., 125
Niebuhr, Reinhold, 79, 88
Noah, 127
Nuclear warfare, 41

Offertory Procession, 133 n., 153
Onan, "onanism," 23 f.
Once-born, the, 58 ff., 69–73, 79
Ontological, 10 ff., 46, 49, 144
Oriental religions, 67
Original Sin, 74 f., 96 f.
"Orthodoxy," 29, 33, 39, 123, 132
ousia, 34, 121 f.
Oxford Movement, 145

Pantheism, 76, 100
Passover, 63
Paul, St., 28, 61, 69, 72, 119 n., 124; Saul, 61
"Pauline privilege," 46 f.
Pax, the, 133 n., 153
Pelagianism, 52
Penance, 149
Perennial philosophy, the, perennial, 34, 39, 42, 83
persona, person (of the Trinity), 34, 110, 121 ff., 125 ff., 138 f., 152
Personalities, types of, 11, 58 ff., 67
Peter, St. 124
Pharisees, 109, 116 f.
Phillips, J. B., translation of the Bible, 133
Philosophy, 18 f., 32, 69, 119, 140
Pietism, 54, 93 f.
Pilate, 117
Pittenger, W. N., co-author of The Faith of the Church, 148
Plausibility, 11, 19–21, 58, 75–77, 84 f., 99 f., 111, 126
Polity, 11, 24, 54 f., 132, 145 ff., 150; see also Holy Orders; Succession, historic
Polygamy, 45
Polytheism, 15 f., 83, 120, 123
Prayer, 40, 45, 53, 64, 71, 87 f., 95, 98, 100 f., 106 f., 108, 136–38
Precepts of the Church (Roman Catholic), 37
Predestination, 68, 85, 137

Pre-existence of Christ, 111, 126 f.
Presbyterianism, 29, 47 n.
Priesthood, as Holy Order, 55, 150
Proof, see Logic
prosopon, 121 f.
Providence, 99 f., 105 f.
Psychology, psychoanalysis, 14, 47, 61, 80, 92 f., 95, 128 f., 133
Public disasters, 82, 86, 102

Race relations, 38 f., 72, 89, 94 f., 104 f., 110, 117
Real Presence, the, 33, 54, 106
Reason, see Logic, Plausibility
Reconstruction, theological, 8, 10, 120, 132
Redemption, see God as Redeemer, Salvation
Reformation, the, 62, 144, 149
Reformed Church in South Africa, 30 n.
Reformed tradition, 29, 149, 153; see also Presbyterianism
Religious freedom, 42, 89
Remarriage after annulment or divorce, 46 f., 143 f.
Remembering, 62–64, 77, 107
Resurrection, the, 40, 63 ff., 73–75, 77 f., 85, 91, 100, 107, 113, 118 f., 127
Revelation, 100 f., 103, 109 f., 112–115, 125 f., 128; see also God as Revealer
Revolution, theological, 7 ff.
Rhymes, Canon Douglas, No New Morality, 49 n.
Rigidity, see Absolutism
Roadblocks to faith, 13–15, 17–19, 23 f., 79
Robinson, J. A. T., Christian Morals Today, 49 n.; Honest to God, 7–9; and D. Edwards, The Honest to God Debate, 7 n.

Roman Catholicism, 26–
29, 31 n., 37, 40–47, 54,
68 n., 92, 101, 133 n.,
145–47, 149, 153

Sabellianism, 52, 121 f.,
125 n., 152
Sabbath, the, 40. 63, 139
Sacraments, sacramental,
33 f., 44, 53, 48, 56 f.,
69, 100, 107, 147–150;
see also Baptism; Con-
fession; Confirmation;
Eucharist, the; Holy Or-
ders; Marriage; Unction
of the Sick
Sadducees, 116 f.
Salvation, 68 f., **75–77**, 85,
100, 110, 127, 137; see
also Predestination
Sarum rite, 53, 145–47
"Scandal of particularity,"
the, 100, 114
Schizoid tendencies in life,
16, 66
Science, scientific evidence,
17 f., 21 f., 34, 42, 83,
89 f.
Second Coming, 89
Secularism, 10, 17
seder, 63
Sermons, survey of content
of, 37
Sex, 41–45, **47 ff.**, 92, 97,
118
Sh'ma Israel, 94, 138 f.
Sin, 75, 79, **91 ff.**, 106, 149
Slavery, 38
Social conditioning, 11, 23,
32 ff., 43, 63, 75, 81,
92 f., 95–97, 102, 131,
146

Social gospel, 39, 89 f.
Solidarity, human, 75–77,
96 f.; of God and man,
76
South Africa, 30, 110
"Spiritual death," in mar-
riage, 46 f., 143–44
"Sprinkling occasions," 15
Stephen, St., 89
Substance, substantia, 32–
34, 121 ff., 138 f.
Succession, historic, 55 f.,
159 f.
Suffering Servant, the, 77,
91, 113
Suicide, 92 f.
Sunday, 40, 63
"Supernatural," 100, 114
Symbols, 9, 61, 131 f.

Taizé, 153
Taylor, Jeremy, 48, The
Rule and Exercises of
Holy Living, 48
Technology, 89 f.
Temple, Archbishop Wil-
liam, 148; Christianity
and the Social Order, 96 f.
Theresa, St., 69, 72
Thomism, 33 f.
Transfiguration, 127 n.
Transubstantiation, 33
Trinity, the, 34 f., 52,
120 ff., 138, 152
Tritheism, 122 f.
Twice-born, the, **58 ff.**,
69 f., 72 f., 77

Unconscious, the, 66, 92,
96
Unction of the Sick, 27,
54, 149

"Undivided Church," 30
Unitarianism, 108, 123
United Church of Christ,
129 f., 138
United Presbyterian
Church, 47 n.
Unity, Church, 55–57, 138,
148–50; principal plans
for, 56 n.
Usury, 50

Values, see Ethics
Vatican Council I, 55; II,
29 n., 68 n., 149 n.
Verb vs. noun thinking, 39,
121
Vincentian Canon, 31
Virgin Birth, 18, 35, 139 f.

War, 40 f.
Washington Cathedral Col-
lege of Preachers, survey
by, 37
Weber, Max, 85
Western culture, 88–90
Western rite, 145 f.
Westminster Confession,
29, 35
Whitehead, Alfred North,
86
Williams, H. A., Sound-
ings, 49 n.
Word, the, 56, 109–12,
125–27, 139
Worship, 85, 121; modes
of, 11, 24, **51 ff.**, 72, 129,
133, 139 f., 145 ff., 153;
right of, 42

Zealots, 116 f.
Zoroastrianism, 83, 109,
137

INDEX OF SCRIPTURE QUOTATIONS

OLD TESTAMENT

Genesis
1:26 ff. 96
38:8–10 26

Exodus
15:1–2, 13 105–106

Deuteronomy

19:14 133

Job
37:23 76

Psalms
51:5 96
69:23–36 136

95:8–11 136
137:7–9 136

Isaiah
10:5 101
52:13—53:12 ....7 n., 91
55:8 76

NEW TESTAMENT

Matthew
5:48 94
7 22
19:46 46

Mark
2:27 139

Luke
2:52 126
18:1–8 99
18:19 109

John
1:1 ....125 f.
1:9 111
1:14 109
9:3 86
14:12 109
14:28 109
15:4 73
15:5 74
17:21–23 57
20:26 ....119 n.
21:13 ....119 n.

Acts
5 82
14:17 112
15:6–29 124
17:28 ....100, 126

Romans
5:12–19 74
6:3 f. 74
6:5 74
8:22 84
12:2 88
13:13 f. 62

I Corinthians
4:3 f. 93
7 48
7:15 46
7:20–31 38
12—14 67
12:12 f., 27 73
15:11 12
15:20–58 ....119 n.
15:22 74
15:48 f. 74

II Corinthians
4:7 ....3, 33, 36, 141
5:19 109
6:8–10 61

Galatians
2:20 73

Ephesians
3:9 126

5:22 f. ....74 n.

Philippians
2:5 113
2:6b–8 110
4:8 128

Colossians
1:15–17 126
2:9 109

Philemon
1:1 ff. 38

Hebrews
1:1 112
12:5 f. 87

James
5:14 f. 27

I Peter
2:18 38

I John
1:1–4 65

Revelation
3:20 106
12:7–12 ....128 n.

Pike, James
  A Time for Christiam
  Candor

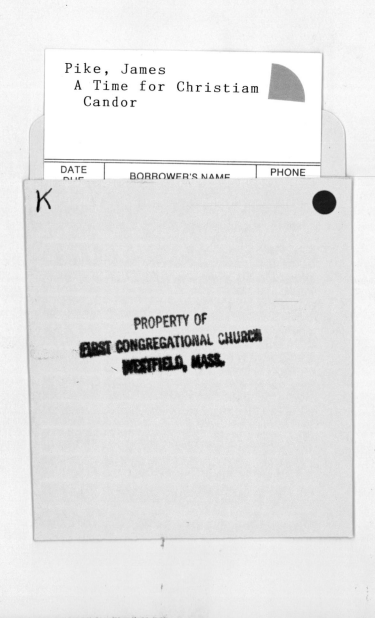

DATE DUE	BORROWER'S NAME	PHONE

K